THE ALLEN
ILLUSTRATED GUIDE TO
SADDLERY

THE ALLEN ILLUSTRATED GUIDE TO
SADDLERY

HILARY VERNON

J.A. ALLEN

© Hilary Vernon 2004
First published in Great Britain 2004

ISBN 0 85131 869 X

J.A. Allen
Clerkenwell House
Clerkenwell Green
London EC1R 0HT

J.A. Allen is an imprint of Robert Hale Limited

British Library Cataloguing in Publication Data
A catalogue record for this book is available from the British Library

Design and make up by Paul Saunders
Illustrated by Maggie Raynor
Edited by Jane Lake
Typesetting by Textype, Cambridge

Colour separation by Tenon & Polert Colour Scanning Limited, Hong Kong
Printed by Midas Printing International Limited, China

I would like to dedicate this book to my Godfather
Gordon Vlies who always took a keen and loving interest in me,
an uncle who I loved and deeply respected.

Contents

Acknowledgements

My thanks to all at E. Jeffries for being so helpful, for allowing me to use the photographs from their new catalogue and for some technical help; to Monty and Suzanna who own Belstane Marketing for their support; to Caroline Burt of J. A. Allen for her continued faith in me; to Kit Houghton for the photograph on page 96; to Smith Brothers, PO Box 2700, Denton, TX 76207, USA – tel: (800) 433-5558, www.smithbrothers.com – for the Western photographs on pages 28, 57 (bottom right), 67, 76 (bottom), 91 (top), 103 (top) 111 (bottom), 120 (bottom left); to Rodeo Dave Charnley (Trick Rider) for the Western photographs on pages 73 and 120 (bottom right); to Patricia and Victoria Spooner for the side-saddle photographs on pages 91 (bottom), 92, 93, 94, 95, 103, 106, 107, 112 (bottom), 113 (top); and to Sylvia Stanier for the side-saddle photograph on page 112 (top).

1. Riding Bridles

With bridlework and saddlery, as with all things in life, in general you get what you pay for. If you buy inexpensive leatherwork it will not last or look smart for long and in some cases may be unsafe to use even when new.

What style of bridle you choose and what sort of noseband and reins you use will be dictated partly by individual taste and partly by which equestrian sport you are participating in and how much control you need to apply when you are riding your horse.

Bridlework This is normally manufactured in three widths ½ in, ⅝ in and ¾ in. Which width you choose should be dictated by the make and shape of the horse or pony you are riding or driving. For instance, for the neat small head of a lead-rein pony, a show pony or an Arab you may consider ½ in bridlework because wider heavier bridlework will look too clumsy and detract from a pretty face.

For a larger pony or small horse, ⅝ in bridlework will look much better and more in proportion.

A large hunter or cob type could have ¾ in bridlework because the head of such a substantial horse would look too large in narrow bridlework.

Bridlework colours Traditionally bridlework was always London tan in colour. Nowadays the most commonly seen colours are havana and black.

Showing classes traditionally have brown (havana) bridlework and saddlery.

Polo bridlework has traditionally always been London tan. The sport of polo is a strong contact equine sport and needs substantial bridlework and saddlery for safety and durability.

TO FIT It is very important that your horse's or pony's bridle fits comfortably and correctly. A badly fitting bridle can be dangerous and can also cause evasions which are often thought to be related to the bit but which are, in fact, simply a case of the horse not being comfortable with the fit of his bridle.

With the bridles in this chapter, the headpieces, browbands and cheekpieces are fitted in a standard way, as follows. Where there are exceptions to the rules, they are listed under their respective bridles.

The headpiece should lie just behind the ears over the top of the head. The splits (where the leather is cut to form the throatlatch and the cheekpiece) should be level with the base of the horse's ear, or just a little lower. If the split is higher than this then, where the throatlatch bends backwards to go under the horse's jowl, as the split opens, the browband is pushed up onto the base of the horse's ear. The throatlatch should be fitted so that you can get approximately three finger widths between the side of the horse's cheek and the throatlatch when it is done up, so that the horse can flex the throat and jowl area without any restriction.

I have read two theories on the sizing of the actual crownpiece that fits directly over the top of the horse's head. One theory is that the horse's head is not very wide where the crownpiece sits and therefore, in order to sit comfortably, the crownpiece should be no more than an inch wide with the throatlatch a separate part. The saddler is then able to reduce the size of the crownpiece and the bridle

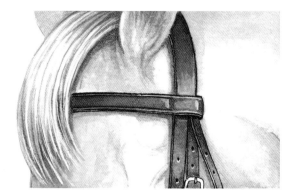

Langham Reed headstall

will not be forced forward onto the back of the horse's ears. There is a pattern of headstall, called the Langham Reed headstall, which was designed to allow the crownpiece to sit comfortably back from the ear.

The other theory is that the crownpiece should be wider and padded and in one piece so that any downward pressure is more evenly distributed, particularly when using the double bridle because poll pressure is felt by the horse when the curb rein is activated.

I think both theories have a lot of merit and it depends on the individual conformation as to which of the three types of headpiece (splits, separate parts or one-piece) fits a horse best.

bridle crownpiece showing the splits where they should be

KB bridle one-piece crownpiece

The browband should lie on the horse's forehead low enough so that you can fit your index finger between the base of the ear and the top of the browband and should also be long enough so that the same finger can be fitted behind the horse's ear between the back of the ear and the headpiece. The length is very important, if it is too short the headpiece will be pulled forward and pinch the back of the ears. The loop of the browband (where the noseband and the headpiece are pushed through) should be wide enough to allow both pieces of leather to fit.

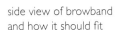

side view of browband
and how it should fit

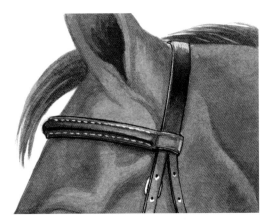

The cheekpieces lie down either side of the horse's face and should be buckled so that they are on the working hole (the working hole is the middle hole, therefore if you have five holes available you will fasten the cheek into the headpiece on the third hole up or down, whichever way you are counting). This should mean that the cheekpiece and noseband buckles of your bridle are more or less in line with the back of the horse's eye. The working hole should really apply to every strap that is buckled on your bridle, so that in the event of an accident and any of your bridlework being damaged you always have an extra hole or two above a possible break.

cheekpiece fastened
on the working hole

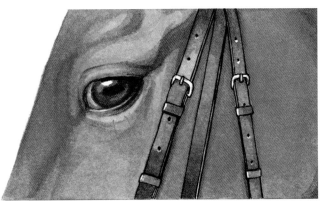

Snaffle Bridles

TO FIT See pages 16 and 17 for the headpiece, browband and cheekpiece fitting details.

The noseband should sit comfortably on the face, whatever the type of noseband used. It should be placed high enough not to interfere with the horse's breathing and low enough to sit approximately two finger widths below the projecting cheek bone. Although some nosebands are designed to fit quite tightly, they must never be so tight that they cause actual harm to the horse. If your horse is

parts of the snaffle bridle

1. noseband headpiece
2. browband
3. headpiece
4. throatlatch
5. noseband
6. bit
7. cheekpiece
8. rein

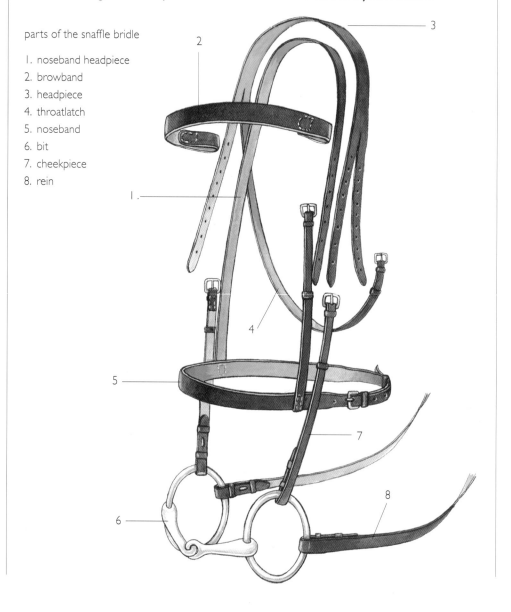

resisting the bit by opening his mouth, a tight noseband will just make him more uncomfortable and not solve the problem of why he feels the need to resist in this way. These three nosebands are all well placed on the horse's face.

far left cavesson noseband

centre flash noseband

above adjustable drop noseband

Snaffle-bridle types

Plain
A plain snaffle bridle would be used for everyday riding as well as Novice Working Hunter Pony, Novice Working Hunter, Novice Hunter and Novice Hunter Pony classes when the schedule requires competitors to present in a plain snaffle bridle. The width of the bridlework and the actual width of the noseband will depend on the size of the horse or pony and the length of his face. The colour of the bridlework is traditionally brown for competitive showing.

Raised stitched
This style of snaffle bridle would be used for everyday riding or, combined with a velvet browband, it would be used for Lead Rein, First Ridden and Novice Show Pony or Novice Riding Horse classes.

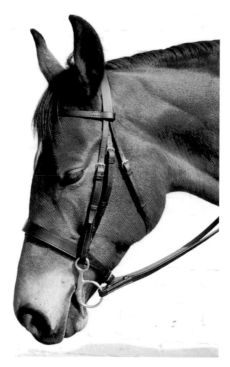

plain snaffle bridle with a plain browband and
plain cavesson noseband

raised stitched snaffle bridle

raised stitched snaffle bridle with a velvet browband

Polo Bridles

These bridles are traditionally London tan in colour, and should always be made of a heavy gauge leather and in ¾ in width bridlework for strength and safety. As the average polo pony ranges from 15 hh to 15.3 hh, the bridlework is always a cob-sized plain pelham or gag bridle with a wide, strong cavesson noseband to accommodate a substantial standing martingale. The nosepiece is slightly wider than the rest of the noseband. The heavy-duty noseband and martingale take considerable strain when the pony is pulled up or turned.

On the polo gag, the cheekpieces are made of either rope or rolled leather but rope is more commonly used. As you apply pressure on the reins, the rope slides much more quickly through the holes in the cheek of the gag bit in order to get a faster result. More importantly, from the horse's point of view, the pressure is also released more quickly. There should be a stop on the gag cheek below the bit to prevent the bit sliding too far down the cheek at the bottom and digging in the horse's mouth. The gag bit actively encourages the pony to carry his head high as the action of the bit lifts the head carriage, but the standing martingale stops it from coming up too high.

TO FIT In principle, all bridles should fit in the same way when it comes to the comfort and fit of the headpiece and browband (see the general **To fit** section on pages 16 and 17). Because the cavesson noseband is wider than usual, it is important to check that it is still lying in the correct position on the horse's face.

polo gag bridle with rolled leather cheeks

polo pelham bridle

Double Bridles

TO FIT See pages 16 and 17 for the headpiece and browband fitting details.

The cheekpieces should, as with the snaffle bridle, be buckled on the working hole, i.e. the middle hole. Because the cheekpieces are the main part of the bridle, they should always carry the Weymouth (the curb bit) as it needs more stability than the bradoon.

parts of the double bridle

1. headpiece
2. bridoon sliphead
3. noseband headpiece
4. keeper
5. bridoon rein
6. fly link
7. curb rein
8. lip strap
9. single-link curb chain
10. low-ported slide-cheek Weymouth bit
11. curb rein-ring
12. lip strap ring
13. plain curb hook
14. loose-ring jointed bridoon bit
15. nosepiece
16. cheekpiece
17. throatlatch
18. browband

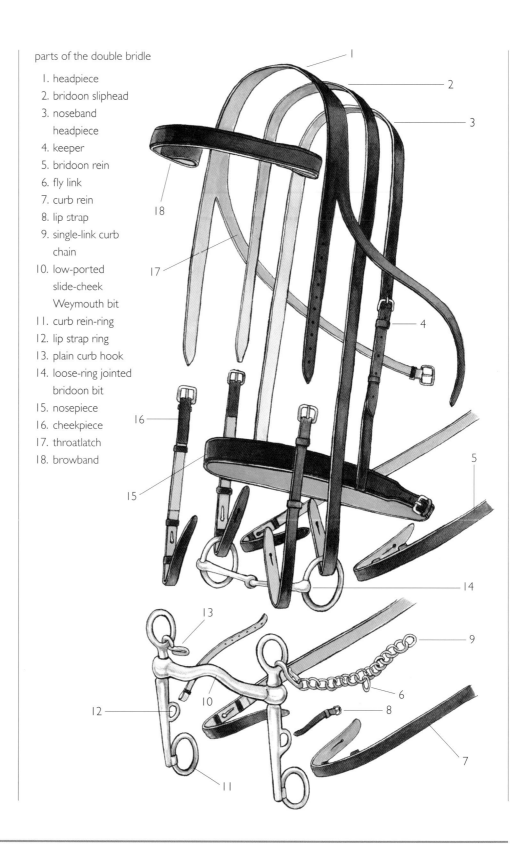

The cavesson noseband is the only type of noseband that should be used with a double bridle. It should fit comfortably, as described on page 18. It is most important that the noseband is not too tight with a double bridle because the horse has two bits in his mouth, which is a lot of metal, and he needs to be able to swallow freely and open his mouth a little to move the two bits comfortably.

The bradoon sliphead should be threaded through the loops on the browband between the headpiece of the bridle and the headpiece of the noseband and should be buckled on the offside. If you buckled the sliphead on the nearside you would unbalance the look of the bridle as there would be too many buckles all one side of the horse's head. By buckling it on the offside, it makes the overall appearance neater and better balanced. The bradoon sliphead should always carry the bradoon bit and never the Weymouth.

The curb chain must be twisted clockwise until it is perfectly flat. As you hook it up to the nearside curb hook, make sure the links remain flat against the horse's jaw. The fly link in the centre of the curb chain must hang down and carries the lip strap.

The lip strap should always be worn with a Weymouth bit; it gives a much more finished and correct appearance and helps to keep the chain flat and in place.

The reins on a double bridle are down to personal choice but if you have small hands two ½ in reins are less of a handful, and if you are worried about distinguishing the top from the bottom rein, maybe a laced rein or a plaited leather rein for the top rein and a plain rein for the bottom rein would help.

Double-bridle types

Plain
This style of bridle would be used for everyday riding, dressage, hunting or Ridden Hunter, Working Hunter, Ridden Hunter Pony or Working Hunter Pony classes.

Raised noseband and velvet browband
This style of bridle would be used for everyday riding or Show Pony, Show Horse, Show Hunter, Riding Horse and Hack Classes.

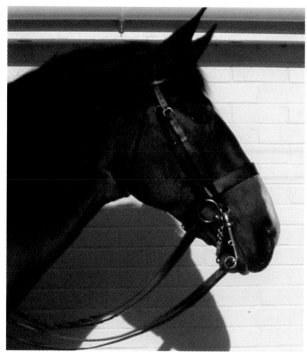

plain double bridle

double bridle with a raised, white-lined noseband and browband

Pelham Bridles

Pelham-bridle types

Rugby

The Rugby pelham would be used if the effect of a double bridle was needed but the horse or pony could not be ridden in two bits. This style of bit should be put onto a double bridle and, if fitted correctly, will look like a double bridle until it is inspected closely. The floating 'bradoon' ring is attached to the bradoon slip-head of the double bridle. With a pelham, the same styles of bridlework apply to the classes for which you would normally use a double bridle, e.g. a plain bridle for hunter classes and a raised stitched bridle with a velvet browband for show classes.

Pelham

This style of bridle would be used just as the above if for some reason the two bits of the double bridle or the Rugby pelham could not be used. An ordinary pelham bit, i.e. a pelham with a solid cheek not a floating ring like the Rugby pelham, would be fitted onto a snaffle bridle but a second rein would be added so that the top rein would act as the 'bradoon' and the bottom rein would act as the 'Weymouth' and when used would bring the curb chain into play.

Rugby pelham on a plain double bridle

Rugby pelham on a raised stitched double bridle with a raised stitched browband

TO FIT

The headpiece should lie just behind the ears over the top of the head, the splits (where the leather is cut to form the throatlatch and the cheekpiece) should be level with the base of the horse's ear. If it is higher than this, where the throat-latch bends backwards to go under the jowl, as the split opens the browband is pushed up onto the base of the horse's ear. The throatlatch should be fitted so that you can get approximately three finger widths between the side of the horse's cheek and the throatlatch when it is done up, so that the horse can flex the throat and jowl area without any restriction.

The browband should lie on the horse's forehead low enough so that you can fit your index finger between the base of the ear and the top of the browband and also be long enough so that the same finger can be fitted behind the horse's ear between the back of the ear and the headpiece. The length is important because, if it is too short, the headpiece will be pulled forward and pinch the back of the ears.

The cheekpieces should be buckled on the working hole (the working hole is the middle hole so if you have five holes available you will fasten the cheek onto the headpiece on the third hole which will be exactly the middle hole) this should apply to every strap that is buckled on your bridle.

The cavesson noseband must sit comfortably on the face whatever the type and be placed high enough not to interfere with the breathing and low enough to sit below the projecting cheek bone. Although some nosebands (for example the crank cavesson) are designed to fit quite tightly, they must never be so tight that they cause actual harm to the horse.

The lipstrap should always be worn with a pelham bit because it gives a much more finished and correct appearance and helps to keep the curb chain flat and in place.

The reins on the pelham bridle are down to personal choice but if you have small hands two ½ in reins are less of a handful. If you are worried about distinguishing the top rein from the bottom rein, maybe a laced rein or a plaited rein for the top rein and a plain rein for the bottom rein would help.

The Rugby pelham should always have a **bradoon sliphead** which should be threaded through the loops on the browband between the headpiece of the bridle and the headpiece of the noseband and should be buckled on the offside. If you buckle the sliphead on the nearside you will unbalance the look of the bridle, as there will be too many buckles on one side of the horse's head. You should attach the floating rings of the Rugby Pelham to the bradoon sliphead so that you create the appearance of a double bridle while only having to use one bit in your horse's mouth.

Western Bridles

Although certain bridle styles have become accepted for particular classes at Western shows, in general the choice of style is down to what suits the horse, the rider's preference, the job to be done, and, often, the dictates of fashion. Both snaffles and straight-bar and ported curb bits are used with Western bridles.

Working bridle

This bridle is used for many different aspects of Western riding: ranch work, pleasure riding, reining, cutting and training young horses. A browband and throatlatch on the bridle make it more secure on the horse's head, particularly if young horses are being trained or the faster more vigorous activities of reining and cutting are being indulged in.

Show bridle

This bridle would be used for Western Show, Western Trail and Western Pleasure classes. A show bridle often has one or two ear loops instead of a browband, usually has no throatlatch, and is often highly decorated with fancy leatherwork and silver. The amount of decoration must be chosen carefully because it can sometimes overwhelm a horse's head rather than complement it, and the judge will be looking at the overall appearance.

working bridle

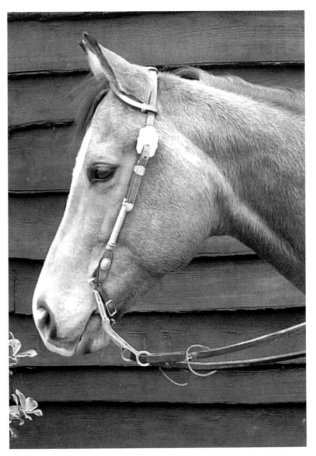

show bridle

TO FIT As with all bridles, the comfort of the horse and the safety of both horse and rider are of paramount importance. Although Western riders work with a looser contact than English riders, the bit must still lie in the correct place just wrinkling the corners of the horse's mouth. The browband must be large enough not to pull the headpiece forward onto the back of the horse's ears, and a throatlatch should have three finger widths between it and the side of the horse's cheek when it is done up.

The ear loops on the one-ear and two-ear bridles must be large enough to allow the ears to slip comfortably through them and must not rub the base of the

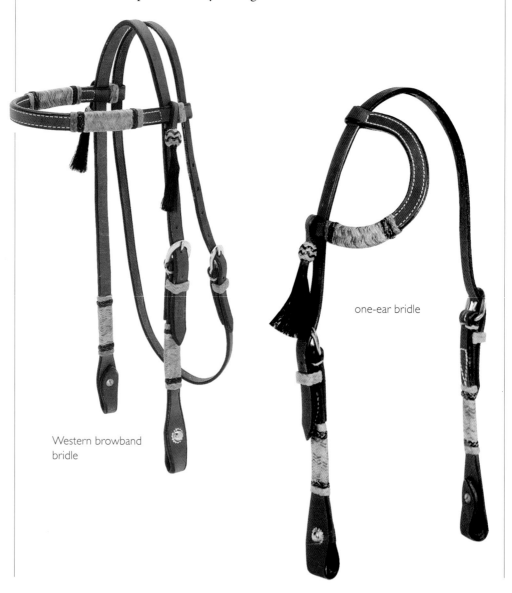

one-ear bridle

Western browband bridle

ear. There are two types of ear loops, the 'loose' and the 'fixed'. The loose loops are made separately and have looped ends, which slide over the headpiece. The fixed loops are incorporated into the headpiece and are either narrow slots or slits, or wider shaped loops.

Most Western bridles do not carry a noseband unless a tiedown is required, then a cavesson-style noseband is used and the tiedown attaches to the back of the noseband.

2. Combination Bridles

Norton or Citation

This bridle has two mouthpieces, one a loose-ring, thin-jointed overcheck, the other a loose-ring jointed bradoon. The cheekpieces of the bridle attach to the rings of the overcheck. The reins attach to the rings of the bradoon. Around the mouthpiece of the overcheck are two metal fixtures that carry a nosepiece. This is potentially quite a severe bridle, combining very thin snaffle mouthpieces with nose and poll pressure. As the reins are used, the cheeks of the overcheck are pushed into the side of the horse's face and the two jointed bits arc in on the horse's tongue forcing it in to the triangle created by the two bits. The more the bit pulls back in the mouth, the more nose and corner lip pressure is brought to bear. If the bridle is correctly fitted, the horse should start to respond to the action of the nosepiece before the bits really begin to apply severe pressure.

TO FIT Fit the bits into the horse's mouth high enough into the corners to just cause a wrinkle and you should be able to place your index finger on each side of the horse's face between the corner of the lips and the bit rings. The nosepiece should be snug against the horse's nose to avoid pulling the bits forward in the mouth and fitted as high as possible so as too interfere as little as possible with the horse's breathing.

Norton or Citation bridle

Newmarket

This bridle has a jointed Wilson snaffle with a leather nosepiece attached to the floating rings; the nosepiece is supported by small straps which are connected to the cheekpieces of the bridle so that it cannot drop down too low and interfere with the horse's breathing. This bridle is most effective when used with two reins so that when the snaffle rein is used the bit acts as a snaffle with the added severity of the floating rings pushing in on the sides of the horse's face. If you use the rein that is attached to the floating ring you activate the nosepiece of the bridle before the action of the bit. If the bridle is correctly fitted, the horse should start to respond to the action of the nosepiece before the action of the bit.

TO FIT Fit the bit comfortably into the corners of the horse's lips. Then adjust the nosepiece so that, when the rein is attached to the floating ring, more pressure is transferred to the nose. In a less severe form the nosepiece is attached to the front of an ordinary snaffle; when the nosepiece is tightened you can relieve a lot of pressure on the mouth. The nosepiece can be adjusted on both forms to transfer the pressure from the mouth to the nose or a combination of both in differing degrees.

Rockwell

The Rockwell uses the same type of nosepiece as the Citation but has only one bit. It is usually a loose-ring jointed snaffle, but you could have a snaffle with a medium port or a mullen mouth. The nosepiece fits onto the bit in the same way; it has two rings that attach to the metal fixtures of the mouthpiece that lie between the corner of the horse's lip and the cheek of the bit. The nosepiece is adjustable so that the rider can apply more or less nose pressure as the rein is used. As the rein is taken up, the bit is pulled back in the mouth and the action is on the corners of the lips, the sides of the tongue and the nose if a jointed snaffle is used, and more on the middle of the tongue and then the bars of the mouth and the nose if a mullen mouth is used.

TO FIT The bit must be the right size for the mouth because the rings of the nosepiece sit right next to the corners of the lips and too narrow a bit would certainly cause rubbing. The nosepiece should sit as high as possible on the nose without pulling the bit up in the horse's mouth. The nosepiece should be adjusted to apply pressure just before the bit does.

Newmarket bridle

Rockwell bridle

Myler Combination

The Myler combination is designed to distribute the signals given to the horse. As the rein is activated, the cheek of the combination turns and the nosepiece of the combination gives firm pressure onto the front of the nose, then the jaw strap presses into the upper jaw and finally, as the cheek keeps turning, pressure is felt on the poll. This gives the horse three very clear signals to slow down and tip the face inwards before the bit is activated in the mouth. Only as you continue to use the rein and the mouthpiece of the bit slides around to the stop on the cheek, does the horse feel any bit pressure.

Myler combination
bridle

TO FIT Put the Myler combination onto your bridle just as you would an ordinary bit and fit the mouthpiece of the bit comfortably into the corners of the horse's lips. You will not need any other noseband on the bridle. The combination nosepiece must be done up firmly so that it stays in place but not too tightly. If it is too loose, the front of the nosepiece will lie too low on the horse's nostrils and could impair his breathing.

Combination Nose Bridle and Bit

This combination is often an American gag with a hackamore front attached, thus giving the combined effect of a gag plus strong nose and poll pressure. The bridle must be of good quality because badly made versions tend to have the nosepiece far too long causing the nosepiece to drop too far down the nose causing severe discomfort.

TO FIT As with all bridles using frontal downward nose pressure, the nosepiece must not be fitted too low and, as with all bridlework that relies on all-round nose pressure, a careful check needs to be made constantly of all pressure points for possible bruising and rubbed places. The bridle that carries a bitless nosepiece usually needs to have shorter cheeks than a bridle carrying a conventional bit to ensure that the nosepiece lies at the correct height. The bit should fit neatly into the corners of the mouth following the principles of fitting a loose-ring snaffle and the nosepiece should sit comfortably on the face above the soft fleshy part of the nose, not on the nostrils.

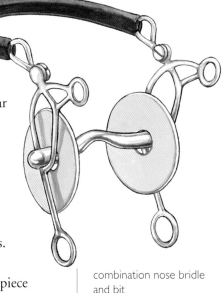

combination nose bridle and bit

Scawbrigg Bridle

The Scawbrigg is a simple form of bitless bridle. It is made of a padded nosepiece usually lined with chamois leather or sheepskin. The nosepiece is supported by a small piece of leather attached to the cheek of the bridle which helps to prevent the nosepiece from dropping too low onto the horse's nose and interfering with his breathing. The back of the bridle has a wide jaw strap which is also padded and rests on the horse's jawbones. The reins are the extensions of the jaw strap which pass through the rings of the nosepiece. There should be a

Scawbrigg bridle with bit

Scawbrigg bridle without bit

supporting strap fastening at the back passing through a loop on the chinpiece to stop the noseband twisting round.

TO FIT The nosepiece should be fitted approximately three finger widths above the nostrils to ensure that the action does not interfere with the horse's breathing. The bridle can also be used in conjunction with a bit. The bit is attached to a bradoon headpiece which will have to be attached unconventionally by running it over the top of the bridle secured in between the browband loops and the head piece. The nosepiece must be the closest thing to the horse's face and if the bradoon headpiece is fitted conventionally under the headpiece of the bridle, the nosepiece will press the cheekpieces that carry the bit into the horse's face. A separate pair of reins is used for both the nosepiece and the bit so that you can carefully work the horse between bit pressure and nose pressure in varying degrees.

3. In-hand Bridles and Accessories

In-hand Bridle

The in-hand bridle is designed for male horses or ponies that are shown in-hand, not ridden, and which have to be shown in a bridle with a bit. This would apply to a gelding over the age of three, a colt over the age of a year or a stallion. Mares are usually shown in riding bridles. An in-hand bridle would be used with a single rein that usually buckles to the centre ring of a chain or leather coupling attached to the bit. This gives control by means of even pressure on both sides of the horse's mouth.

in-hand bridle

Couplings

Newmarket chain

A Newmarket chain is usually made of brass to match the fixtures on an in-hand bridle used for showing. It has a Walsall clip at each end and a round link in the middle to which you attach the lead rein. They normally come in two thicknesses: the heavyweight chain is for larger animals and the lightweight chain is for much smaller ponies to match the narrower bridlework.

TO FIT The Walsall clips attach to the bit rings on each side of the snaffle or metropolitan bit (an in-hand bit) and lies under the horse's chin. The leather lead rein buckles onto the ring in the middle of the chain.

Newmarket leather coupling

This coupling is made of leather instead of chain but still normally has brass fittings. The two leather straps are joined in the middle by a brass ring and two ends buckle round the bit rings.

TO FIT Buckle the coupling under the horse's chin to each side of the bit with the buckles facing downwards, then attach the lead rein to the ring in the centre.

Newmarket chain

Newmarket leather coupling

Heavy leather tee coupling

This coupling is very substantial and would be used for a large colt or a stallion.

TO FIT The tee coupling buckles on to each side of the bit and on to the back of the noseband of the bridle; as you pull on the lead rein the action is distributed between the mouth and the nose of the horse which is a help if you have a strong colt and you do not want to pull continuously on the mouth. The lead rein attaches to the brass ring in the middle of the tee.

Brass chain and leather lead rein

The chain and lead rein is often used by attaching the chain to one side of the bit passing it under the chin through the other bit ring to the handler's hand. As the handler pulls the lead rein, the chain tightens under the horse's chin. The only problem with using the chain in this way is that any pressure directly under the chin, especially a chain which gives quite a bite, has a head-lifting effect on the horse rather that a steadying slowing effect.

TO FIT It is better to attach the chain to a Newmarket or tee coupling rather than under the chin, as you will have more control over the animal.

heavy leather tee coupling

brass chain and leather lead rein

Conversion accessories

Bit snaps

These are used to convert a leather headcollar into a bridle by attaching a bit to it. They have either a brass or steel finish to blend in with the stainless steel or brass cheek of a bit, or the headcollar fittings.

TO FIT Clip the snap onto the headcollar first so that the fastening faces the outside. This is important; if you were to fasten the bit snap inwards there is a chance that the horse may get his lip caught in the snap. Finally snap the bit into place.

Bit straps

These are used for the same purpose as the snaps but are small leather straps which also have stainless steel or brass buckles to complement the bit cheek or tack.

TO FIT Fasten the bit onto the headcollar so that the buckle of the strap is on the outside and the point of leather faces downwards.

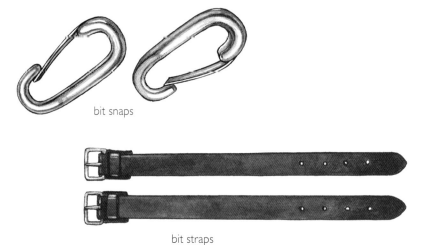

bit snaps

bit straps

4. In-hand Restraint

We are often at our most vulnerable when leading our horses, especially if small and light in stature and leading a large horse, or if the horse is difficult to lead. It does not take a bright horse very long to realize that we cannot control him if he really puts up a concerted effort to escape from us in a headcollar. Simple tasks such as walking our horses to and from the field can become quite frightening. The following pieces of equipment are specifically designed for in-hand work and do not require a bit, thus making it easier to remove the restraint from the horse's head without the added risk of him throwing his head up and getting the bit caught on the front teeth or lower jaw and therefore creating an additional problem of anticipating something painful when being turned out in the field.

Restrainer Noseband

This leading device is used to great effect on strong youngstock, stallions and difficult-to-lead animals. It has a well-padded nosepiece with a sprung-steel core and crossover straps which pass behind the face and attach to an ordinary lead rein or rope. It is used in conjunction with a headcollar. As the lead rein is pulled, the cross straps tighten the sprung nosepiece and firm pressure is applied to the nose, as soon as the horse stops pulling and the handler regains control and loosens the pull on the horse's head, the pressure on the nose is released.

restrainer noseband

TO FIT The restrainer noseband is fitted to the noseband rings (or squares) of a conventional headcollar using bit straps or snaps. The headcollar is fitted high on the horse's face so that the restrainer is at the height of a drop noseband; if fitted lower, it would interfere with the horse's breathing.

Be Nice Halter

This restraint and training device is for use when leading and training your horse in close in-hand work. The halter is made of a very smooth, good quality type of thick cord which slides easily through the metal parts of the device. It works on the principle of instantly applied firm poll and nose pressure. As the horse resists, you pull down on the rope attached to the halter and the device tightens on the nose and the poll. As soon as the horse complies and the handler slackens the rope, the pressure is instantly released. It is made of nylon and Dacron braid, which is very soft, strong and pliable and easily tightens and releases through the metal rings. Over the horse's poll area there are smooth cast-bronze bobbles that push down into the horse's head just behind the poll to reinforce the downward signal.

TO FIT There are four American sizes all geared to western-sized horses (Quarter Horse/cob-sized) so it can be quite an art to pick the right size for your horse. Take in a headcollar that fits your horse well when you go to purchase a Be Nice halter so that you have a good measurement guide.

Be Nice halter

5. Bitless Bridles

It must be remembered that most bitless bridles and hackamores are designed for the more Western approach to riding which means the rider signals the horse with the reins, the horse obeys and the rider relaxes the rein pressure which is the horse's reward and the indication that he has done as he has been asked. This type of bridle does not work if the equipment is fitted too high on the horse's face and if the rider continues to ride with an unrelenting pressure on the rein; the horse gets no relief from the pressure and is therefore never rewarded. And, as with any uncomfortable restriction, the horse will eventually find a way to carry the pressure more comfortably by evading it.

The nosepiece should lie just above the horse's nostrils so that when pressure is applied by the rein, the nosepiece drops onto the top of the nostrils and starts to impair the breathing. As the horse comes back to the hand and the rider relaxes the rein, the nosepiece rises up and removes the pressure.

Myler Hackamore

The Myler hackamore is designed a little differently from the hackamore or bitless bridle patterns with which we are familiar. The nosepiece of the hackamore is set on to the front of the cheek at a lower angle than the jaw strap. This means that as you use the rein, and the cheek of the hackamore turns, the first thing that the horse feels is nose pressure. With most of the other patterns of hackamore the first pressure the horse feels is jaw pressure. Under-jaw pressure alone causes the horse to lift the head up, whereas nose pressure first followed by poll then jaw pressure gives the horse very clear slowing and stopping and head-lowering signals.

Myler hackamore

TO FIT The Myler is fitted so that the nosepiece lies on the horse's nose just above the nostrils, not directly on the nostrils. As the rein is used and the cheek turns, some downward pressure will, however, be applied over the nostrils until the horse lowers his head, relaxes and slows the pace, then the pressure is released.

Blair's Pattern Bitless Bridle

This bitless bridle works on leverage. As the rein is used, the cheek turns, the jaw strap moves against the upper jaw of the horse and, as the cheek continues to be turned, downward pressure is brought to bear on the front of the horse's nose. This type of bitless bridle has reasonably good stopping ability but has very little turning power.

TO FIT The nosepiece and hackamore cheeks are fitted onto a conventional bridle without a noseband. You may find that, as the cheek is long, you may need to use a shorter cheekpiece on your bridle. Care must be taken to fit the nosepiece high enough so that when in use it does not drop too low and interfere with the horse's breathing.

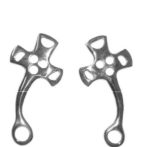

Blair's Pattern bitless bridle

BR Equi Bridle

This bitless bridle works on a sliding pulley system. As the rein is used, the two pulleys are drawn up the cheeks putting pressure simultaneously on the nose and on the poll. The pulleys are prevented from sliding too close to the eyes by clips attached to the nosepiece. It has a potentially very strong action and needs a lot of padding at the back of the nosepiece.

·BR equi bridle

TO FIT Again, the nosepiece must be fitted high enough to ensure that when in use it does not drop too low and interfere with the horse's breathing. The leather and chain noseband must have a rubber curb guard between the horse's jaw and the curb chain, or some similar padding to prevent the bridle being too severe. Just as you would fit a curb chain, the chains must all be twisted flat so that they lie comfortably on the horse's face.

Side-pull Hackamore

This Western bridle comprises a headpiece, cheekpieces and a browband attached to a double or single rope-fronted noseband or a leather-covered rope noseband. The reins attach to rings on each side of the horse's face at the back of the nosepiece. The idea of this form of bridle is that a young horse can be firstly long-reined and then ridden from the nose. All the formative training of young horses begins with control on the nose, they are already accustomed to this form of control. The horse can then be long-reined again from the nose with the addition of a bit attached to the bridle. The bit is held in the mouth without any use being made of it initially. Then, as a rider is added to the equation, the young horse is ridden first from the nose only and then with an extra rein attached to the bit. Gradually less nose pressure is used and more bit pressure so that the work flows through and is clearly understood by the horse.

TO FIT To emphasize the point again, any head device that relies on nose pressure must not interfere with the horse's breathing so must be sufficiently high on the nose not to touch the fleshy nostrils but not so high as to rub the projecting cheek bones. The noseband should fit the nose snugly so that there is minimal side-to-side movement as the reins are used.

Bosal

The *bosal* is the original, true Spanish hackamore (*jaquima*) taken into the New World by the *Conquistadores* and favoured by the Californian *vaqueros*. It works by applying pressure to the front and side of the nose and to the underside of the jaw. The braided rawhide nosepiece (bosal) ends in a fashioned knot (heel knot) under the jaw. A soft, thick hair rope (*mecate*) is attached by being wrapped around the bosal just above the heel knot and forms the reins and a lead rope. The combined weight of the heel knot and the mecate acts as a counter balance to the heavy nosepiece. Some hackamores consist solely of the bosal,

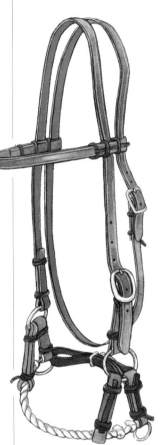

side-pull hackamore with single rope-fronted noseband

mecate and the headstall but others might also have a *fiador* and/or a browband. The fiador is a throatlatch that also attaches to the heel knot to regulate its position and stop it bumping against the horse's jaw when he is working.

The head carriage is controlled by the horse's head movements being finely balanced between the nosepiece and the heel knot. When the rider's hand is raised, the lightest restraint asks the horse to bring his head in, or 'tuck' in. If he raises his head too high, the nosepiece comes into contact with the nose to correct the head position. Should the horse try to evade this by overbending, the heel knot applies pressure to the jawbones. Initially, the reins are held in both hands to give directional aids: one hand takes the rein out to the side in the direction required and the other hand lays the opposite rein against the horse's neck. When the reins are held in one hand, the horse is neck-reined. All rein aids must be given simultaneously with weight, seat and leg aids.

TO FIT The bosal must be adjusted so that, when the horse's head carriage is correct, only the cheeks of the bosal have a light contact with the horse's face, neither the nosepiece nor the heel knot should be applying pressure. The balance and fit of the bosal can be adjusted by adding or removing wraps of the mecate. The bosal should lie about 2 in above the nasal cartilage, and the cheeks of the bosal should slope downwards, at an angle of about 45 degrees, towards the curb groove, with the heel knot lying below the curb groove.

the bosal

6. Bridle Accessories

As well as considering which bridle is going to be correct for your horse and any competitions you may enter, there is also a large range of bridle attachments and accessories to consider if the bridle is to fulfil its task and the horse is to be correctly turned out and completely comfortable. It is no good getting the colour of your bridlework and the shape of the noseband and browband right if the corners of the lips are being pinched by a badly fitting curb hook, or your bradoon sliphead is put on incorrectly, which will lose marks in a Tack and Turnout class.

Curb Chains

Single-link curb chain
Little seen these days, this type of curb chain is not as comfortable for the horse as the thicker double-linked variety.

Double-link curb chain
This is the chain that is issued with nearly all curb-chain-carrying bits these days. They come in four standard sizes: small pony, pony, cob and full, though, if necessary, chains can be made longer than the standard full size.

single-link curb chain

double-link curb chain

Flat-link, or polo, curb chain

The flat links cover more surface area than the ordinary single-link variety and this chain is therefore more comfortable because it spreads the pressure load. The only possible drawback is, on a horse with a very narrow curb groove, the chain may cause too much pressure on the more sensitive upper curb area.

Jodhpur curb chain

This is a severe curb chain; the large, shaped central link moves the pressure from the less sensitive curb groove, right onto the very sensitive jaw area where the mandible nerve runs down the jaw line with only a very thin layer of skin for protection. This brings to bear severe pressure over a large area and must cause the horse pain if used carelessly.

TO FIT All-chain curb chains must be twisted so that the chain lies completely flat on the horse's jaw. You must hook the chain onto the offside of the bit then twist it clockwise until it is flat, as you hook it onto the nearside of the bit make sure it remains flat in the curb groove. The small fly link must hang down at the bottom of the chain so that the lipstrap can be threaded through it. An excessive number of spare links can look untidy dangling from the side of a bit. The excess links can be nipped off with pliers providing that enough are left for adjustments to be made. It is correct when using a curb chain on a driving bridle to cut off the fly link, as a lipstrap is not used on a driving bit.

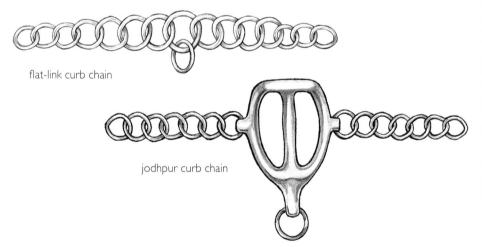

flat-link curb chain

jodhpur curb chain

Leather curb chain

A very much kinder alternative to chain, it evenly distributes the pressure in a continuous strip, but requires more maintenance as the leather needs to be kept soft and supple all the time. They are usually made in a fairly thick leather but saddlers can make them up in soft bag hide on request.

Elastic curb chain

This is an even softer alternative than leather. The stretch in the elastic is an added bonus for a very sensitive horse; as the curb strap comes into play the give in the elastic allows more time before the full action of the curb is felt by the horse. Again, it must be kept clean so that the horse's saliva does not make the elastic strap go hard thus causing the curb-groove area to be rubbed.

TO FIT As with the all-chain curb chains it is important that the three or four links of chain at each end of the leather or elastic strip lie flat on the horse's skin. Twist the offside links straight then fasten the curb onto the offside of the bit. Make sure the leather or elastic lies with the curve, wrapping comfortably around the horse's curb groove, and then twist the remaining links at the near end and fasten to the nearside of the bit.

leather curb chain

elastic curb chain

Curb Guards

Rubber

This is a very effective and inexpensive way of helping to soften the effect of a chain, the chain must be twisted to flatten it out then the rubber curb protector slides over the flattened chain, once encased the chain has to lie flat. They come in several colours but black and brown blend in well with the leather of bridlework.

Gel

This very soft flat leather pouch is filled with gel to buffer the effect of the curb chain, and lies comfortably against the horse's skin. Made in soft, supple, fine leather, it enables the chain encased by the guard to mould to the shape of the horse's face, and must be cleaned and oiled regularly to keep it supple. To put the gel curb guard on to the chain, twist the chain flat and then thread it through the loops at the back of the guard so that the chain lies flat and the fly link threads through the little slot in the middle of the central loop.

TO FIT If the whole curb chain is twisted straight before being threaded through the guard, the guard will help keep it flat, but it is also important that the three or four links of chain at each end of the guard lie flat on the horse's skin. Twist the offside links straight then fasten the curb chain onto the offside of the bit making sure the smooth side of the guard lies against the horse's skin wrapping comfortably around the horse's curb groove. Then twist the remaining links at the near end and fasten them to the nearside of the bit.

rubber curb guard

gel curb guard

Flat, or Circle, Curb-chain Hooks

The metal of curb-chain hooks usually supplied with a bit can be inferior to the metal of the bit itself and frequently they are not very well made. The flat curb-chain hook is of much better quality and lies more comfortably on the side of the horse's face; there is a lot less risk of the corner of the lip being pinched. You can buy these separately and fit them to the bit yourself.

TO FIT Remove the existing hooks from the bit and then hook on the flat curb-chain hook making sure that the flat sides will be against the horse's face and that the hooks face to the outside.

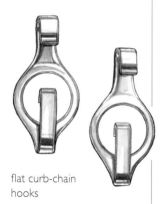

flat curb-chain
hooks

Lip Straps

This small leather strap helps to keep the curb chain in place and also prevents the cheeks of a Banbury pelham or Banbury Weymouth from rotating too far. They come in either a flat or rolled pattern and are available in colours to complement your bridlework.

TO FIT Attach the lip strap to small eyelets sited on the cheeks of either a pelham or a Weymouth bit. With a pelham, the eyelet lies in between the bradoon rein ring and the curb rein ring. With a Weymouth, the small eyelet lies just above the rein ring. Make sure that you run the lip strap through the fly link which is the small extra link that hangs down in the middle of the curb chain.

rolled lip strap

Pelham Roundings

If you are unable to use a pelham bit with two reins, roundings connect the top bradoon ring and the bottom curb ring so that just one rein can be attached to the back of the rounding. This means there is an even pull on the bit with very little curb action.

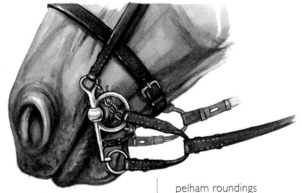

pelham roundings

TO FIT If your roundings are fastened by a buckle then the buckle must face the outside, if fastened by a billet then the billets face the inside. Fasten the roundings onto your pelham bit with one end on the top bradoon ring and the other end on the bottom curb ring. This will then create a D shape to which your reins are fastened.

Fulmer Keepers or Guides

These small leather loops hold the cheeks of the bit in place by anchoring them to the cheekpieces of the bridle and also stop the bit cheeks going into the horse's nostrils. The keepers create a minimal amount of poll action. These are usually used only on Fulmer snaffles because on this particular bit the rein ring is fitted loosely on to a small arm that protrudes from the back of the cheek, which makes the cheek dip forward when attached to the bridle, unless it has support. These keepers can also be used on other cheeked snaffles although they have much more stability than the Fulmer as the rein rings are actually attached directly to the cheeks.

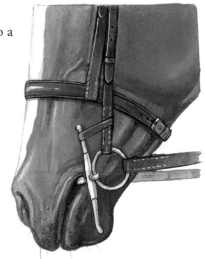

Fulmer keepers should show on the outside of the cheek, not be hidden on the inside

TO FIT Slide the Fulmer keeper onto the lower part of the cheekpiece over the first loop of leather but not over the actual billet. Then fasten the cheekpiece onto the bit and put the other end of the keeper over the top of the cheek of the bit.

Australian Cheeker

This rubber accessory pulls the bit up towards the roof of the mouth to help prevent the tongue from being put over the bit. It attaches to the top of the bridle headpiece with a small strap. As the bit is pulled back in the horse's mouth the nosepiece pulls back on the horse's nose creating nose pressure helping to reinforce the action of the bit.

TO FIT The bit rings are passed through the holes in the middle of the round bit guards with the central strap facing upwards. This central strap then runs up the middle of the horse's face and is buckled onto a small strap attached to the middle of the horse's bridle headpiece.

Latex

This thin self-sealing latex bandage was originally designed as leg protection for American racehorses racing on wet synthetic racetracks because it does not absorb any moisture. In England it is now more commonly used as a wrap for bits. It gives a soft rubbery layer to a bit without making the bit very thick and bulky, which is very useful if you feel a horse would benefit from a rubber-covered bit but know that he probably has not got enough room in his mouth

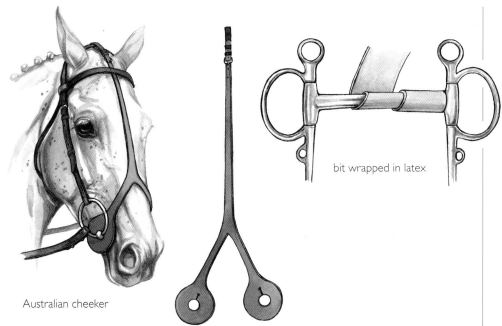

Australian cheeker

bit wrapped in latex

bradoon sliphead

for a thick bit. Care should be taken as latex is not completely smooth and can cause soreness in some horses. It can also be used to wrap in a figure-of-eight pattern on the cheek of a slide cheek bit to stop the play in the cheek or prevent pinching.

TO FIT The latex must be wrapped evenly and tightly so that the bit is the same thickness all the way along and that the layers are firm and do not twist or move. You can cut strips off to fit difficult places as long as the overall thickness is the same. When you have finished wrapping the bit, hold the latex-covered part in your hands because the heat of your skin will seal and mould the latex to the bit.

Bradoon Sliphead

This leather strap carries the bradoon bit of the double bridle; it has billet fastenings to hold the bit and a single buckle to do it up. Some people put the Weymouth bit onto this sliphead; this is incorrect as it is most important that the Weymouth, because it works on a leverage principle, should be on the most stable part of the bridle, which is obviously the main part of the bridle. As the Weymouth applies poll pressure this would mean that, if it is attached to the bradoon sliphead, the smallest part of the bridle is pushed down into the top of the horse's head with no support from the other parts of the bridle.

TO FIT The cavesson noseband of the double bridle should be the piece of leather directly next to the horse's head, then the bradoon sliphead and then the headpiece of the bridle. In order to balance the bridle, the bradoon sliphead should be buckled up on the offside of the horse's head so that there are not too many buckles all on the same side.

Flash Converter

This is usually made from leather and fits over the centre of a cavesson noseband to turn it into a flash noseband.

Flash converter

TO FIT Put the leather flash converter over the centre of the cavesson noseband so that the slots are vertical and line up with the slots at the back of the piece. Then you thread a flash strap through the lined up slots and slide it into position. The buckle of the flash strap is best fastened on the side of the horse's nose, not under the chin, and the flash strap fits below the bit.

Martingale Stop

A martingale stop is essential to the function of the running martingale and an important safety factor.

TO FIT Put the martingale neckstrap onto the martingale itself and then gather the body of the martingale and one side of the neckstrap together. Place the rubber martingale stop over the end of the three pieces and slide the stop along them until it can be fitted over the neckstrap where it joins the chest strap. This keeps the martingale in place and prevents the chest strap from hanging down dangerously between the horse's front legs.

Rein Stops

Rein stops prevent the rings of the running martingale from sliding along the rein and getting caught up in either the buckle on the reins or on the bit itself.

TO FIT Slide one stop onto each rein from the buckle end of the rein as it is less bulky and easier than working from the bit end. They should sit on the reins approximately six inches from the bit end of the rein. The ring of the martingale must lie between the rein stop and the rider's hand.

martingale stop

rein stops

Noseband and Poll Guards

These are designed to prevent the bridle rubbing the poll or the nose areas. Some nosebands are done up so tightly these days that the horse needs to be as comfortable as possible while wearing his tack.

Bit Guards

Rubber bit guards are very useful for stopping the side of a bit from pinching the corners of the lips but they are not accepted in all disciplines. They come in a variety of colours from conventional brown and black to rainbow colours.

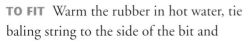

bit guard

TO FIT Warm the rubber in hot water, tie baling string to the side of the bit and thread both bit guards over the string. Tie the string onto an overhead hook and pull each bit guard over the bit rings or cheeks in turn. This is by far the best way as forcing them over the side of a bit with long cheeks with a household spoon is almost impossible, and very hard on the fingers. For presentation driving harness, patent leather bit guards can complement the turnout; these are slit at the side for easy fitting.

Bristle bit guards

These are designed to fit on only one side of the bit. The bristles encourage a reluctant horse to turn in a particular direction. If the horse is bad about turning

noseband and poll guards on a bridle

right, the bristles are fitted on the left, and vice versa, thus making the horse move away from the discomfort. It is very easy to damage the skin on the face with the bristles.

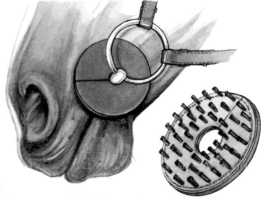

bristle bit guard

Tongue Layer

A tongue layer loops around the bit and lies on the tongue, pointing up the horse's mouth towards the back of the throat, to dissuade the horse from putting his tongue over the bit. Made of black rubber, they can be moved out of position by a determined horse and then possibly chewed.

Tongue Grids

Used on a bradoon headpiece and fitted above the bit, the grid lies on the tongue and, because of its shape, it is impossible for the tongue to be drawn back and over the bit. Made of wire and only in one size, a tongue grid is really a last resort for an habitual tongue problem.

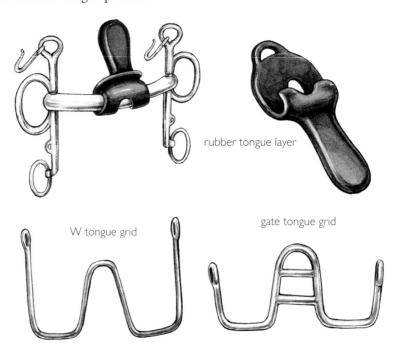

rubber tongue layer

gate tongue grid

W tongue grid

7. Reins

Rein Widths

Reins are manufactured in three widths: $\frac{1}{2}$ in, $\frac{5}{8}$ in and $\frac{3}{4}$ in. Which you choose is mostly down to preference but a child or a lady with small hands will probably be more comfortable with $\frac{1}{2}$ in or $\frac{5}{8}$ in. A man with much larger hands will most certainly need $\frac{3}{4}$ in reins when using a bridle with a single rein.

When riding with two reins in either a double bridle or a pelham bridle on a neat show pony or an Arab you may consider $\frac{1}{2}$ in reins for the bradoon rein and the Weymouth rein, or $\frac{5}{8}$ in for your top rein and $\frac{1}{2}$ in for your bottom rein. A large hunter ridden by a man could have $\frac{3}{4}$ in for a top rein and $\frac{5}{8}$ in for a bottom rein.

Two things will dictate what width reins you choose. The first is, as mentioned above, the size of your hands and what feels comfortable to hold and use effectively, and the second is what effect you are trying to create. A substantial horse is going to look completely wrong in $\frac{1}{2}$ in bridlework and at the other end of the scale, a tiny first-ridden pony is going to look out of proportion with $\frac{3}{4}$ in width bridlework.

Plain Reins

Plain reins are, just as the name suggests, completely plain leather with nothing added to aid the rider to grip the rein in wet weather.

Rubber-grip Reins

These are plain reins with a length of pimpled rubber tubing sewn onto them in a continuous strip for approximately the middle half of their length. These reins are also manufactured in the main in three widths $\frac{1}{2}$ in, $\frac{5}{8}$ in and $\frac{3}{4}$ in. Again, the width you choose will be down to preference and the sort of animal you are riding. As with all bridlework, they are made in different colours to match the colour of the leather of your bridle and saddle but, also, the rubber itself can be in a whole variety of colours other than black and brown.

Continental Reins

Continental reins are made of leather and webbing. Half the rein, from the bit to midway, is made of leather and the hand grips are made of 4- or 5-cord continental webbing. The hand parts have leather bars sewn onto them at intervals so that they are easier to grip. They are good reins in wet weather as they do not slip through the hands. Continental reins can also be made of either all leather or all webbing.

Laced Reins

These reins are made of plain leather which has had thin leather strips laced through the hand part of the reins to improve the grip for the rider.

Plaited Reins

These reins are made of plain leather up to the hand part, then the leather is divided and plaited to make the hand part.

Cotton Plaited Reins

Cotton plaited reins were always traditionally used in the wet as they afforded better grip for the rider instead of slippery wet leather but are rarely seen today.

plain reins

rubber-grip reins

continental web reins

laced reins

plaited reins

cotton plaited reins

Western Reins

There are two basic types of Western reins: split and joined. The split reins are simply two separate reins. Joined reins have a length of leather (romal) at the end. Reins for specialist activities, such as roping or barrel racing, are in one piece. Western reins are longer than English reins – up to 8 ft – and can be made of flat or rolled leather, braided leather or rawhide, cotton cord, cotton rope, nylon parachute cord, webbing, or other manmade materials. They clip, buckle or lace onto the bit.

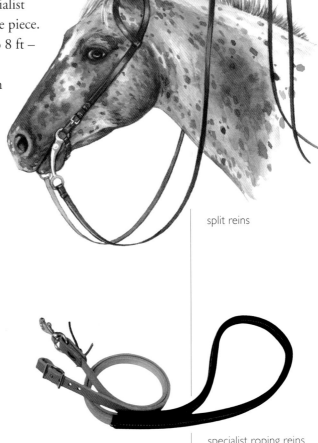

split reins

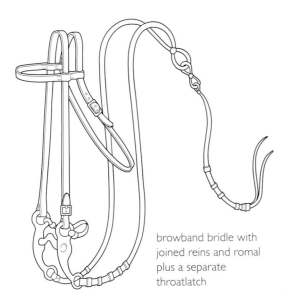

browband bridle with joined reins and romal plus a separate throatlatch

specialist roping reins

Side-saddle Reins

The side-saddle horse wears his usual bridle, although the reins should be a generous length because the hand position of the rider is further back than is normal when riding astride. Reins that are too short will affect both the position and security of the rider.

8. Nosebands

Plain Leather Cavesson Noseband

In its most simple form, this is just a straight band around the horse's nose attached by a headpiece to the bridle. Different widths can be used to good effect; a narrow or a rolled nosepiece will complement a very fine delicate head, whereas a wide nosepiece on a long face, can give the impression of a much shorter head. A wide band strategically placed can also improve a nose with a bump or a dip in the wrong place. ·

TO FIT If fitted only for cosmetic effect the band should lie two finger widths below the projecting cheek bone and you should be able to get two fingers

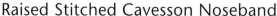

cavesson noseband

between the band and the nose. Fitted a little lower and fastened tighter, the cavesson can discourage the horse from opening his mouth too wide to evade; for this use, a wider padded band should be used to distribute the pressure more evenly.

raised stitched cavesson noseband

Raised Stitched Cavesson Noseband

The raised stitched cavesson noseband has just the same function as the plain leather cavesson but is not as wide and will look more pleasing on a smaller or more delicate head.

TO FIT The band should lie two finger widths below the projecting cheek bone and you should be able to get two fingers between the band and the nose.

Crank Noseband

This noseband has several different names and slight variations of make but the principle is the same. The band is well padded and if made correctly should fit the individual horse. The strapping actually doubles back on itself enabling it to be tightened potentially very severely. When circumstances dictate that a flash or drop noseband cannot be used, for instance with a double bridle, this noseband firmly fastened will help to dissuade the horse from opening his mouth to evade.

TO FIT The fit will be the same as for the cavesson noseband. The padding on the nosepiece should almost meet when the noseband is done up to the required tightness, so that the thinner non-padded tightening strap does not touch the horse. Extra padding can be put behind the noseband where the pressure is greatest to prevent rubbing.

crank
noseband

Flash Noseband

This is really a cavesson with a detachable lower strap designed to allow a standing martingale to be fitted onto the cavesson part if required. The lower strap can be fitted quite tightly to dissuade a horse from opening his mouth too wide.

TO FIT Again, this noseband should be fitted like a cavesson, but high enough so that the lower strap does not interfere with the horse's breathing. To have any effect, both bands must be fastened quite tightly. If you are relying on a tight noseband every time you ride, you must make sure that the horse is not getting rubs or calluses from the constant pressure. The lower strap should be done up on the side of the nose and not directly under the chin as this is much more comfortable for the horse.

raised stitched flash
noseband

Drop Noseband

If fitted correctly, the drop noseband closes the mouth more effectively than any other aid. As the horse opens his mouth to evade, a lot of nose pressure is brought to bear which encourages the horse to drop his nose and relax his jaw to relieve the pressure. Care must be taken in the fitting of the drop; I have always had drop nosebands specially made. The ones usually available in tack shops are too long at the front of the nose, and the buckle end of the back strap can often also be too long while the strap end is too short, making it impossible to fit correctly. The best 'shop bought' ones are the fully adjustable style that can be altered either side of the nose. The most severe form of drop is the polo rawhide drop noseband which works on the same principle but the front piece of the noseband, instead of being a solid leather strip, is made of plaited rawhide which is obviously a good deal more severe than the usual patterns.

TO FIT The drop should be fitted with the front of the band above the nostrils on the solid part of the nose and not on the soft fleshy nasal cartilage. The back strap should angle down below the bit and do up between the chin groove and the corner of the lip, to avoid any pinching.

drop noseband

fully adjustable
drop noseband

Grakle Noseband

This noseband is an effective aid for upper and lower jaw pressure working on a larger overall area than a lot of other nosebands, but it is not accepted by all disciplines. There are several different patterns of Grakle; the only one that works as originally intended is the one that adjusts on the nose (the straps can be moved through the nosepiece and are not riveted into place). By moving the straps through the nosepiece you are able to alter the pressure of the noseband up and down the face.

Grakle
noseband

TO FIT The top strap should be fitted high, pulled up by the noseband headpiece but not high enough to be able to rub the projecting cheek bone. The bottom strap should slant down to fit below the bit and fasten on the side of the horse's nose like a lower flash strap, not under the chin where it may pinch.

Mexican Grakle Noseband

The Mexican Grakle provides a rather severe form of upper and lower jaw pressure working on a larger overall area than a lot of other nosebands.

Mexican Grakle noseband

TO FIT The top strap on this particular Grakle is, in my opinion, fitted too high. It actually rests on the horse's projecting cheekbone which cannot be comfortable. It is also very close to the horse's eye. The bottom strap should slant down to fit below the bit and fasten on the side of the horse's nose, again, like a lower flash strap but not under the chin where it may pinch.

Kineton Noseband

The Kineton relies on quite severe nose pressure; as the bit is pulled back in the mouth some of the pressure is transferred to the nose as the noseband pulls across and down on the nose. This often works well because the formative training of young horses relies solely on pressure on the nose. There are several patterns of Kineton on the market. One allows for extra adjustment on the nosepiece itself. The original Kineton pattern had a piece of metal set into the nosepiece for more severe pressure. The nosepiece attaches to the metal loops which fit under and inside each side of the bit. This noseband should only be used with a snaffle bit.

Kineton noseband

TO FIT The Kineton is fitted like a drop noseband: the nosepiece should lie on the nose bone not on the nostrils. The metal loops fit inside the bit rings and under the mouthpiece on both sides of the bit.

Bucephalus Noseband

Below are two versions of the same principle. As the bit is used the band is pulled back on the front of the horse's nose. The horse feels encircling nose pressure as well as pressure from the bit both inside the mouth and on the chin groove, in the case of a bit with a chain. This noseband is used with pelham and curb bits.

TO FIT Both versions are normally secured to the middle of a cavesson noseband with a small strap, the Bucephalus noseband then lies on the horse's face and the straps go below the bit, crossing over under the chin, and hook onto the curb hooks of the bit. A version with hooks instead of D rings can also be hooked to the floating rings on a Wilson snaffle or into the top eye of a pelham or curb bit.

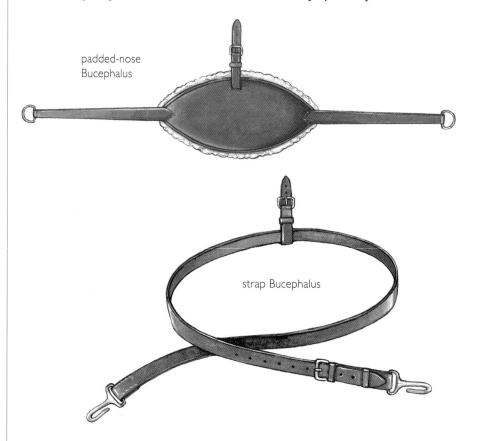

padded-nose Bucephalus

strap Bucephalus

Gillard or Double Noseband

The Gillard is basically a cavesson noseband with a drop noseband sewn below it. Designed to be placed low down on the horse's face, it restricts the horse's breathing to a certain extent and gives very firm pressure when the mouth is open to encourage the horse to lower his head, close his mouth and relax his jaw to relieve the pressure.

TO FIT Fitted lower than the conventional cavesson noseband, it lies about three finger widths below the projecting cheek bone so that the lower nosepiece rests on the top of the horse's nostrils.

Worcester Noseband

This noseband has been specifically designed to allow the rider to apply degrees of nose pressure by using the reins. It is a wide, padded cavesson noseband with a crank-style fastening enabling the nosepiece to be fastened very firmly thus dissuading the horse from opening his mouth very wide to evade the action of the bit. On the front of the band is an additional nosepiece sewn into two sections that angle down and fasten onto the front of each side of the bit, these straps are adjustable to enable more or less nose pressure to be brought to bear. It also seems to encourage the horse to drop the nose to a certain extent.

TO FIT Fit the Worcester like a conventional cavesson noseband: the nosepiece lies on the horse's face two finger widths below the projecting cheek bone but no lower as the drop section must obviously not interfere with the horse's breathing.

Gillard noseband

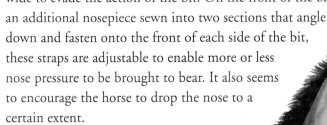

Worcester noseband

Cross-chain Noseband

Potentially a very severe noseband, the cross-chain can be used on a strong horse to good effect by a very experienced event rider. The action dissuades the horse from opening his mouth wide and, in particular, crossing the jaw. As the horse tries to open his mouth to resist there is very considerable pressure from the crossed chains on the back of the jaw, the only way the horse can alleviate this pressure is by closing his mouth and dropping his nose.

TO FIT Although the front of this noseband has the appearance of a drop nosepiece, it should be fitted above the bit. The two chains are crossed at the back of the noseband and are to be fastened snugly but not overly tight.

cross-chain noseband

Scawbrigg Noseband

This noseband consists of a thickly padded nosepiece that adjusts on the front of the nose. The shape is similar to an adjustable drop noseband. A chinpiece passes through two rings at the back of the nosepiece and at each end of the chinpiece are rings for the reins. This can be used as a bitless bridle or you can use a combination of bit and rein by attaching the Scawbrigg to a bradoon sliphead on a conventional bridle and the bit to the cheeks of the bridle. With a rein on the bit and a rein on the Scawbrigg the rider can apply bit and nose pressure in varying degrees.

Scawbrigg noseband

TO FIT Using a conventional bridle, this should be fitted on the horse's head high enough so that the nosepiece does not interfere with the horse's breathing and adjusted so that it fits snugly against the face before the reins are taken up. When used with a bit the nosepiece should be next to the horse's face attached to a bradoon sliphead and the bit should be attached to the cheekpieces of the bridle. Fitted in this way, both the noseband and the bit have separate reins and the rider uses a combination of nose and bit pressure to maintain control.

Combination Noseband

The combination noseband has a short frontpiece attached to a vertical metal cheek and two straps at the back, one lying on the upper part of the jawbone and the other lying in the curb groove. The best pattern has an adjustable front. It is designed for its very definite jaw-closing qualities. As the horse resists by trying to open his mouth or cross his jaw, great pressure is felt both in the curb groove and on the more sensitive upper jaw area. As the horse lowers his head and closes his mouth, pressure ceases, thus dissuading the horse from trying to constantly open his mouth to evade the action of the bit.

TO FIT The nosepiece should fit at the level of that of a drop noseband, up on the nose above the nostrils without interfering with the horse's breathing. The upper back strap should be fastened so that you can get one finger between the face and the band. The lower strap fastens below the bit and, again, you should be able to fit one finger between the strap and the horse's jaw.

combination noseband

Gloster Noseband

The Gloster can be used in five different ways to achieve very specific results. The noseband is a cavesson, with a padded dropped nosepiece incorporating a sprung-steel core sewn into the nosepiece front. The lower piece has an encircling design with rings to which to attach a pair of reins.

1. For a horse that carries his head very high or has a tendency to rear, a standing martingale can be attached to the bottom nosepiece rings. As the horse raises his head too high or tries to rear, the nosepiece is tightened by the martingale and creates nose pressure, the pressure continues until the head comes back into an acceptable angle of control when the pressure is released immediately.

2. Draw reins can be attached to the lower rings so that a top rein is used on the bit and the draw reins act on the lower part of the nose. Skilful application will allow the rider to use the draw reins independently or to work the horse between the two reins.

3. A neck strap can be attached to the lower nosepiece and fastened firmly around the upper neck about two hands breadth behind the ears. This helps to dissuade the horse from trying to lower his head to buck. As the head is

lowered, pressure is brought to bear on the back of the upper neck and also on the lower nose, as soon as the head is raised, pressure is released.

4. If for some reason no bit is required, the headpiece of the noseband can be slipped off and the noseband can be fitted to a conventional bridle headstall, the reins then attach to the lower rings and you have a bitless bridle.

5. It can be used with two sets of reins so that one set is on the bit and a second set is on the lower rings so that the horse can be worked between the two reins creating more or less nose pressure as required.

TO FIT The Gloster is fitted like a cavesson noseband well up on the face but not rubbing the projecting cheekbone. The lower nosepiece is adjusted to lie on the

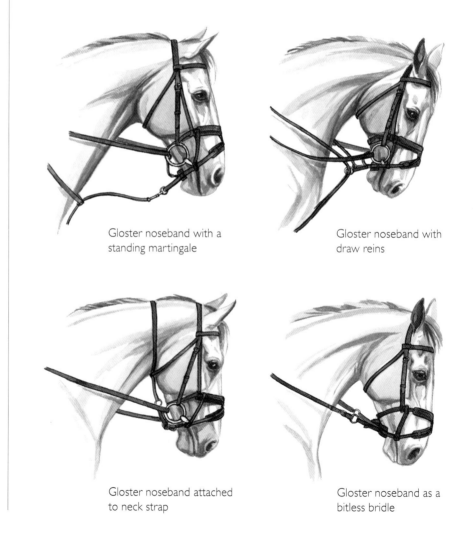

Gloster noseband with a standing martingale

Gloster noseband with draw reins

Gloster noseband attached to neck strap

Gloster noseband as a bitless bridle

nose bone, not on the soft fleshy nostrils, so that it does not interfere with the horse's breathing, and is fastened firmly below the bit but not overly tightly. The supporting straps between the upper and lower bands should be adjusted to lie on the horse's face in front of the bit. The rein rings hang below the lower nosepiece to have either, reins, draw reins, martingale or neck strap attached to them.

Tiedown Noseband

This noseband is for use with a Western bridle when a tiedown is required to help keep the horse's head down. These nosebands come with a ring fitted at the back to take the clip of the tiedown. An ordinary cavesson noseband could be used but the tiedown would then have to have a loop to fit over the noseband.

TO FIT A noseband used with a tiedown must fit like a cavesson and lie about two finger widths below the cheekbone and not so low that it will cut off the horse's breathing.

tiedown noseband

9. Martingales

Running Martingale

The running martingale is designed to prevent the horse lifting his head too high and therefore out of the angle of control; it relies on the tension of the reins to be effective. Attached to the girth by a loop, it passes up between the horse's front legs and divides into two straps at the upper chest, each strap has a ring on the end through which the reins pass. So that the martingale does not hang down and possibly interfere with the horse's front legs, the strap is held in position by a neck strap. A rubber martingale stop should be fitted to prevent the neck strap sliding up and down the actual martingale, and rein stops should be fitted to each rein to prevent the rings of the martingale getting hooked up where the reins join the bit.

There is another pattern of running martingale that does not need a martingale stop: the Lord Lonsdale running martingale. This martingale is cut so that the upper leather part, where the martingale splits to make the rein straps, is much wider just above the neck strap so that it is too wide to slide through the neck-strap loop.

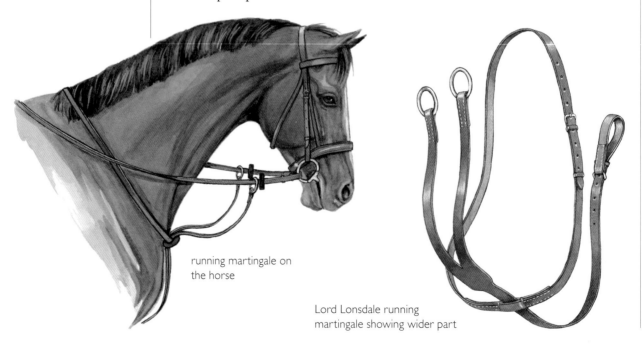

running martingale on the horse

Lord Lonsdale running martingale showing wider part

TO FIT Correctly fitted, the running martingale should only take effect when the head is raised very high and/or the head becomes difficult to control, if it is too short there will be a constant downward pressure on the bars of the mouth. A guide to the correct length is: when the martingale is in place, but not yet attached to the reins, you should be able to take the straps that attach to the reins to one side and stretch then as far as the horse's withers.

Standing Martingale

The standing martingale is also designed to prevent the horse from raising his head too high and therefore becoming difficult for the rider to control. But, instead of relying on pressure on the horse's mouth, it puts pressure on the nose. This device should only be secured to a cavesson noseband or the cavesson part of a flash noseband and never to the dropped part of any other noseband. The martingale is attached to the girth by a loop and comes up between the horse's front legs to attach to the back of a cavesson noseband. Again, as with the running version, to prevent the martingale strap from dropping dangerously low between the horses front legs it passes through a neck strap, which should be fitted with a martingale stop, to hold it in place.

standing martingale attached to a noseband

TO FIT When the martingale is on the horse, place a hand below the martingale strap between the noseband and the neck strap; you should be able to lift the martingale strap into the angle of the horse's throat if it is the correct length.

Cheshire Martingale

Rarely seen these days, this martingale is a combination of a hunting breastplate and the type of standing martingale that attaches to the bit. It applies downward pressure on the bars of the mouth if the horse's head is raised very high.

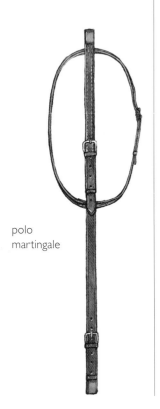

TO FIT The breastplate should be fitted comfortably so that there are three finger widths between the neck strap and the horse's neck and a further three finger widths between the horse's chest and the strap that runs from the girth to the neck strap. The martingale strap should be long enough so that, when attached to the bit, the strap if pulled up will reach into the angle of the horse's throat, as with a running martingale. The martingale strap divides into two and the bit straps clip to each bit ring below the reins not above them so that they will not interfere with the action of the reins.

Polo Martingale

This standing martingale is reinforced with chrome leather all along the martingale strap that runs from the horse's chest to the noseband. As polo is a fast and vigorous contact sport, all the equipment needs to be very substantially made. This martingale also has the length adjustment between the neckstrap and the noseband (unlike a normal standing martingale which is adjusted between the horse's front legs) to enable quick adjustments to be carried out.

Cheshire martingale

polo
martingale

polo martingale

TO FIT It is normally fitted a little tighter than a standard standing martingale but care should be taken not to overshorten the martingale and thus tie the horse's head into an unnatural angle as his balance will be impaired in fast turns and halts.

Web or Bib Martingale

Designed to fill the dual role of running and Irish martingales, it looks just like a running martingale but a solid piece of leather is sewn into the V made by the rein attachments. The action is still that of a running martingale, pulling down on the bars of the mouth if the head is thrown up or carried too high, but, if the rider is thrown, the bib piece also helps to prevent the reins being thrown over the horse's head and getting caught up in his front feet.

web or bib martingale

TO FIT The fitting is the same as for a running martingale and the effect on the horse will be the same as that of an ordinary running martingale. The immobility of the solid leather part keeps the reins in place fairly close together. This part needs to be kept very supple or it can rub the underside of the horse's neck.

Irish Martingale

The Irish martingale is designed to stop the reins from going over the horse's head in the event of the rider coming off, and is most commonly seen on race horses. It is made up of two rings joined by a leather or web strap approximately 4 in long.

TO FIT The reins are threaded through the rings and the martingale keeps the reins in place just under the horse's neck. This piece of equipment should always have martingale stops

Irish martingale

fitted to each rein so that the rings do not get caught up on the buckle or billet fastenings of the reins where they attach to the bit.

Combination Martingale

This a blend of both standing and running martingales. It is basically a running martingale but where the straps divide there is an extra ring to which is attached a standing-martingale strap.

TO FIT The combination is fitted as a running martingale, with the standing-martingale part adjusted to come into force only if the horse's head is thrown higher than the running part can control. When used on a jumping horse, great care must be taken to ensure that the standing part is correctly fitted so that the horse has enough freedom to jump well.

Tandem Martingale

This is a running martingale that, instead of having just one ring at the point where the martingale attaches to the reins, has a two-point contact. The straps forming the V of the martingale are attached to metal pieces that enable the reins to run through two rings 6 in apart so, instead of the rein being pulled down at one fixed point, the load is spread over a wider area. The idea is that the

combination
martingale

tandem martingale

downward drag on the bars of the mouth is not quite so severe. This also comes with extra rings so that it can be turned into a conventional running martingale.

TO FIT Fit as a normal running martingale but pay special attention to the metal pieces to ensure they do not rub the hair of the horse's neck.

Tiedown

The tiedown is the Western equivalent of the standing martingale and is used for the same reason: to prevent the horse from raising his head too high. The pressure is on the nose, so a cavesson-type noseband or tiedown noseband must be fitted to a bridle that does not have a noseband.

TO FIT The tiedown strap loops over the back of the noseband, feeds down through the D ring in the centre of the breastcollar, runs down between the horse's front legs and clips onto the D ring on the front cinch. Alternatively, some tiedowns loop over the front cinch and clip to the ring at the back of special tiedown nosebands. If a breastcollar is not used, a neck strap will keep the tiedown in place.

the tiedown is threaded through the ring of the breastcollar and attached to the centre D ring of the front cinch and the back of the noseband; note the all-rope bridle and reins

10. Breastplates and Breastgirths

Breastplates and breastgirths are designed to stop saddles from slipping back.

TO FIT Breastgirths and breastcollars have the same design; they fit around the chest and are held in place by a strap that goes over the neck, in front of the withers, and by two straps at the end of the girth or collar that attach to the saddle girth under the saddle flaps. The actual girth or collar must be placed correctly on the chest: if it is too high it will interfere with the horse's breathing, and if it is too low it will interfere with the shoulder action.

Breastplates have a single strap that is attached to the girth and passes up through the horse's front legs. Two straps connected by a ring to the girth strap then go round the horse's neck (one on either side) and attach to D rings, or staples, at the front of the saddle by straps and buckles. The neckpiece of the breastplate should fit along the line where the shoulder meets the neck.

Hunting Breastplate

The hunting breastplate is the traditional breastplate pattern used to secure the saddle safely in place so that it does not slip backwards. You may need to use a breastplate if your horse has large powerful shoulders and is a lot narrower behind the saddle, or if your horse is very fit and athletically lean.

Elasticated Breastplate

This is based on the traditional hunting breastplate pattern but the neckpiece is made of thick elastic. The principle use, however, is the same.

Polo Breastplate or Breastcollar

This pattern of breastplate is very substantially made, as polo is a very fast and vigorous sport that relies on the equipment to keep the polo pony and rider safe. The breastplate is used to keep the saddle forward and in place especially when the very fit pony is galloping flat out.

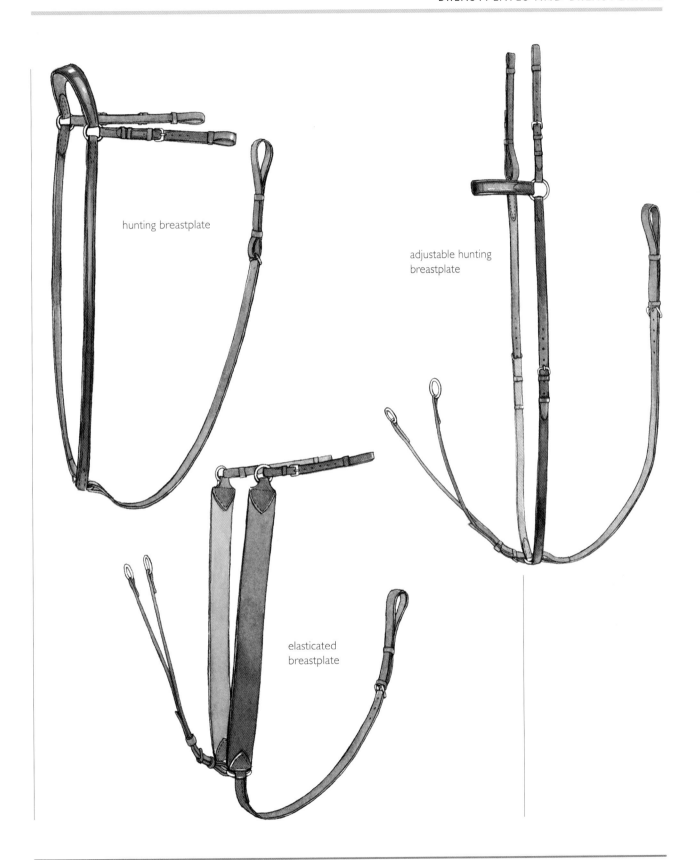

hunting breastplate

adjustable hunting
breastplate

elasticated
breastplate

Elasticated Breastgirth

This breastgirth's pattern originated from copying the breastcollar of a driving harness.

Western Breastcollar

This is used to stop the saddle slipping back on fast-moving roping horses, for uphill terrain and, as with English breastcollars, for horses with the sort or conformation that needs help with keeping the saddle in place.

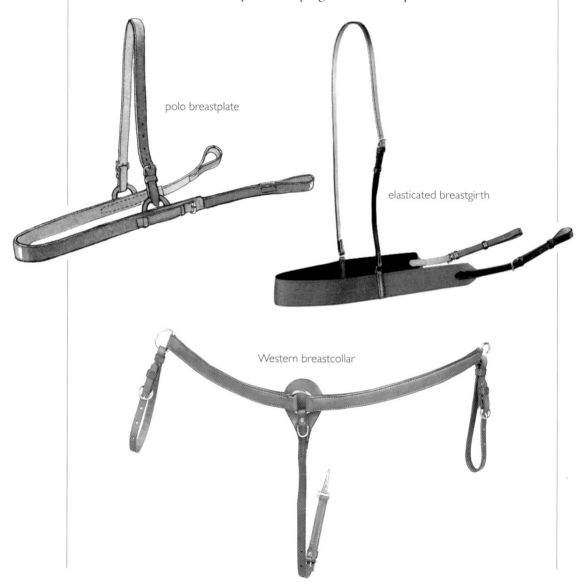

polo breastplate

elasticated breastgirth

Western breastcollar

TO FIT The two shoulder straps of the breastcollar are often contoured or shaped to ensure a good fit along the shoulder, and buckle to the saddle either on the rigging rings or on D rings or slots in the skirt. The central strap runs down through the horse's front legs and clips to a D ring at the front of the cinch in the centre. In the centre of the breastcollar, where the two shoulder straps and the cinch strap meet, there might be a ring to allow for the attachment of a tiedown.

wool breastplate sleeve

Breastplate Sleeves

Some horses are very sensitive to any friction. The constant movement of a breastplate on the horse's shoulders as he moves can sometimes rub the hair off the front of his shoulders and, if not dealt with, can actually make the horse sore. These wool sleeves Velcro round the breastplate to stop any chafing.

11. Saddles

When you buy a saddle it is vitally important to buy a good quality saddle from someone who is properly trained to fit saddles. In the long term this will prove to be good value for money; you will get a product and correct information that will enable you to ride your horse comfortably knowing you are not harming your animal or compromising your own safety.

I think it is very important to get a saddle fitter who is trained and approved by The Society of Master Saddlers. If you go for a cheap option both with the fitter and the quality of the actual saddle and there are subsequent problems, then you will have great difficulty and probably a lot of expense putting things right. Members of The Society of Master Saddlers usually have the Society's crest displayed in their shop and often on their literature. This proof of membership should guarantee good service, quality products and expert advice.

How a Saddle is Made

The tree

The tree is the inner part of the saddle. It is the shape of the tree that determines the shape of the saddle itself, this is called 'the cut'. The jumping saddle is said to be 'forward cut' and the dressage saddle, 'straight cut'.

The tree is usually made from strips of laminated beech wood. The strips are heated and shaped then glued together and covered with a muslin fabric. Steel

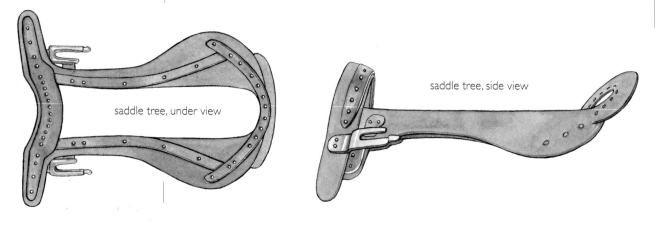

saddle tree, under view

saddle tree, side view

plates are used to strengthen the pommel, or front arch, and the gullet, which is the channel that runs down the middle of the saddle. A half-round cantle plate is attached to the back of the saddle tree to re-enforce the cantle. The finished tree is covered with waterproofing glue. Most modern saddles have spring trees, which simply means two long thin pieces of metal are attached to the tree on either side of where the seat is to be. These provide the tree with a little 'give' so that the seat is more comfortable for the rider and not so rigidly immovable on top of the horse's back. At this stage, the stirrup bars are riveted on.

The Stirrup Bars

The strongest and safest stirrup bars are made of forged steel. In the past, the stirrup bars were very prominent and tended to make the stirrup-leather buckle stick out and press into the rider's inner thigh. These days the stirrup bars are recessed so that the stirrup leather and buckle sit tucked into the saddle under the skirt and this is much more comfortable for the rider. If the stirrup bars are put on too tightly, it is very difficult to put the stirrup leather onto the saddle and may also lead to additional problems when the saddle is flocked-up (stuffed) for the first time.

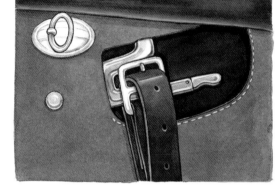

recessed stirrup bar

Today, the positioning of the stirrup bar is crucial if the rider is to be able to adopt the correct seat for the type of riding required. Its placement on the tree is, therefore, dictated by the design of the saddle and the purpose for which it is to carry the rider. The ideal position is one where the rider feels comfortable and in balance with the length of the stirrup required for a specific discipline or sport. A line drawn through the rider's position should go straight down from the shoulder through the hip to the heel.

At the end of the stirrup bar there is a little catch which can be pushed up. In the past, riders were told to push this catch up to stop the stirrup leather from coming off the saddle. I think this is potentially very dangerous and modern-day saddles are designed in such a way that it is unlikely that the leather will come off in everyday riding situations. It is, therefore, safer if the catch is left down.

Now the tree is complete, the saddler has to begin building the saddle around the tree.

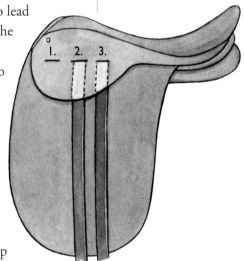

the different positions of the stirrup bar
1. the position of the stirrup bar on a jumping saddle
2. the position of the stirrup bar on a general purpose saddle
3. the position of the stirrup bar on a dressage saddle

The seat

The seat is attached to the tree. The girth straps are attached to pieces of web, which go across the top of the tree. On top of the webbing is placed a comfortable pad to make the seat 'rider friendly'. In the past this would have been serge or wool stuffing but often now it is a dense piece of rubber. The actual leather of the seat can be anything from doeskin to suede or pigskin.

The skirt

The skirt, which is the small leather flap that hides the stirrup bars, is now attached.

The flaps

The flaps are stitched into place under the skirt. Now the top of the saddle is complete.

The panels

A small leather pocket is added to each panel to hold the tree points, and the panels are stitched onto the tree. They are then flocked-up with, usually, wool flocking, carefully and evenly so that the underside of the saddle is lump free.

TO FIT Put the saddle on the horse's back further forward than the position it will eventually lie in, and then slide it back into place to ensure that the horse's coat lies unruffled under the saddle. We tend to place saddles too far forward,

the parts of the topside of a saddle

1. pommel
2. seat
3. cantle
4. flap
5. D-ring
6. skirt

under the flap of a saddle

1. flap
2. girth safe
3. thigh roll
4. girth straps
5. panel
6. knee roll
7. tree points pocket

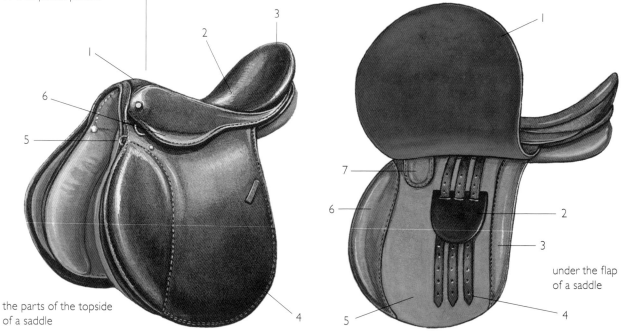

the parts of the topside of a saddle

under the flap of a saddle

even tilted partially up the withers; they should rest comfortably just to the back of the withers. Girth the saddle up so that it sits firmly on the horse's back.

As you look at the saddle from the side it should be in balance: neither too high at the front nor too low at the back; the seat should be level. As a general rule there should be a gap at the front between the underside of the front arch of the pommel and the top of the horse's withers of approximately 2 in with the weight of a rider on the saddle so that the underside of the arch will not press down onto the top of the horse's withers. Stand on a box and look down the gullet of the saddle to make sure it comfortably clears the horse's spine all the way through the middle. The two bearing surfaces of the underside of the saddle should sit on the muscles either side of the spine where the horse can bear the weight comfortably. The back of the saddle underneath the cantle must also clear the horse's spine with an approximate gap of 1½ in with the rider's weight in the saddle. Always ride the horse when fitting a new saddle; it should be comfortable and stay relatively still on the horse's back in all gaits.

The saddle should look in proportion on the horse from the side view. Even if the rider is very small, a large horse is going to look out of proportion in a 16 in saddle that will be too short on the horse's back and will rest in the wrong place, possibly making the back sore. At the other end of the scale, a 17½ in saddle is going to be far too big for a 13.2 hh pony and, because it will be too long, it will rest on the loins, the weakest part of the horse's back.

The saddle is measured from the middle of the cantle to the stud rivet on the top of the saddle on the skirt.

How to Check for Damage to a Saddle

As you are maintaining and handling your saddle, check the stitching on the girth pulls and stirrup leathers, and on the saddle in general.

The tree itself needs to be checked regularly as well, particularly if the saddle has been involved in an accident.

The pommel or front arch

This can be damaged easily if your horse rolls with his saddle on or falls out jumping and rolls over on the saddle. To check for soundness, hold the saddle in both hands and pull the front arch apart, if it widens dramatically as opposed to having just a little 'give', or squeaks or grates, then there will be damage.

The waist or seat

This is the middle of the saddle. The waist of a spring-tree saddle should have a little movement but should not give a lot or make a noise when bent. To check this, hold the pommel in one hand and the cantle in the other and lightly placing your knee in the centre of the seat, push down with your knee and pull up with your hands. Any major movement or cracking indicates a broken tree.

You must be careful when mounting the horse that, as you pull yourself upwards, you do not hold onto the middle of the cantle as this can twist the tree. When you mount you should hold onto the far side of the saddle under the panel and the thigh roll, or over the top of the saddle onto the knee roll. I always use a mounting block, being small and none too athletic! It saves both the horse and me from discomfort and struggle.

Saddle Safety

In my work I visit a lot of different yards, which are, in the main, run very efficiently and safely. But even in the best yards I sometimes see things that I feel are very unsafe. Your saddle is one of the most expensive things you will probably buy, apart from the horse himself, so it makes sense to follow these rules to protect it.

1. Never leave a saddled horse unattended unless he is securely tied as he may roll on the saddle and break the tree.

2. Never let the stirrups down on your saddle until you are just about to get on. Do not lead your horse through doorways or gateways with your stirrups down. Some people seem completely unaware of the terrible danger they place themselves and their horses in. Until you have seen a horse catch a dangling stirrup on a gate or a door and pull the saddle backwards onto his loins with the girth just in front of his hind legs, you cannot possibly imagine the violence that your horse is capable of. He will not stop bucking and running until he has got rid of the saddle and possibly fatally damaged himself and all manner of other things as well.

3. Never loosen your girth so much that the saddle is in jeopardy of sliding around your horse's back.

Jumping Saddles

The jumping saddle should be specifically designed to enable the rider to adopt the correct position for jumping comfortably any size of fence without compromising a good safe position in the saddle or interfering with the ability of the horse to jump freely and naturally.

The saddle normally has a sloped-back head to allow for a more forward-cut panel which, when you adopt a jumping position with a much shorter stirrup leather, helps your body to maintain a forward jumping attitude. Knee and thigh rolls also help the rider to maintain this position.

The jumping saddle is not designed for everyday riding. Some designs are very narrow across the waist, concentrating the pressure over a much smaller surface area on the horse's back. This can lead ultimately to back and pressure problems for the horse if the saddle is used on a daily basis.

Jeffries close contact jumping saddle

Jeffries traditional jumping saddle

Dressage Saddles

The dressage saddle allows the rider to sit in a more upright position so that a comfortable long-leg position can be attained without reaching for the stirrup. This ensures that clear, concise leg aids can be given without excessive extra (and therefore confusing to the horse) movement from the lower leg, and enables the rider to sit with an elegant and useful upper body position.

dressage saddle

The dressage saddle is designed with a straighter panel to accommodate the longer leg line and the stirrup bar is set further back to assist the position. The saddle has a wide bearing surface in order to spread the pressure on the horse's back because in this sport the rider spends more time actually sitting down in the saddle than in most other horse sports. Dressage saddles normally have two long girth straps so that a shorter girth can be used. This buckles lower down than a normal girth so that there are no bulky buckles under the rider's leg.

General Purpose Saddles

The general purpose is the most widely used type of saddle; it is a compromise between a dressage saddle and a jumping saddle and is designed for participation in any general riding activity.

The general purpose saddle is styled with a panel and flap that allow the rider to not only shorten the stirrups to be able to jump a few fences but they are also wide enough for the rider to lengthen the stirrup and adopt a longer leg line for schooling the horse.

general purpose saddle

Working Hunter Saddles

The working hunter saddle is a compromise between a show saddle, which shows off the conformation of the forehand, and a general purpose saddle which enables the rider to jump hunt-type fences. Both the horse's conformation and jumping ability can, therefore, be demonstrated under one saddle in a Working Hunter class.

The saddle is often designed with a cut-back head and straight-cut flaps, but with fairly substantial knee rolls for jumping.

working hunter saddle
with padded knee rolls

Show Saddles

The show saddle is purely for showing off the horse's or pony's conformation, in particular the forehand, enabling the movement of the gaits and the look of the shoulder to be completely unhindered by the knee roll of a saddle.

The show saddle is usually designed with a half panel instead of a full one, a very straight-cut flap and, often, a cut-back head. You certainly have to admire the ability of a show rider to sit a big buck successfully when sitting on a show saddle.

Polo Saddles

The polo saddle allows a polo player to be very mobile when riding the fast stops, turns and sudden spurts, and when leaning right out from the saddle to play the

show saddle

polo saddle

ball while guiding the pony with one hand. It is very important that the saddle is well made because, of all the equestrian sports, polo probably has the most physical contact with other ponies and their equipment. Polo ponies are normally between 14.2 hh and 15.2 hh which means a tall man's centre of gravity is very high over the pony's back. It is, therefore, crucial that he is well balanced in the saddle and that the saddle itself helps the player to maintain his position.

The polo saddle is normally designed with a half panel and is built on an 18 in or 19 in narrow to medium tree so is therefore quite a long saddle when you consider the average size (15 hh) of most polo ponies.

Endurance Saddles

The endurance saddle has to fulfil two roles: it must be very comfortable for the horse to wear for very long periods of time, and it must distribute the rider's weight evenly when he is travelling over all types of terrain and in all weathers. The rider must also be comfortable and able to change position and stirrup length with ease.

The saddles are designed in two styles. One is based on the military pattern of saddle which has a very wide bearing surface and is built on the principle of two long pads either side of the horse's spine joined at the front and back. The modern endurance saddles are mostly based on conventional trees and have padded seats for rider comfort as well as the very wide bearing surfaces for the horse's comfort. The saddles have additional features of extra metal rings at the front and rear so that small pieces of equipment can be carried with ease.

endurance saddle

Western Saddles

'Western' is a very broad term for several different aspects of a particular riding style. The Western saddle evolved to service the needs of both horse and rider to enable them to do the job of working cattle: flushing them from hiding places, cutting them from the herd, roping them etc.

Saddle designs and styles of horsemanship varied according to the type of terrain in which the work was done. For example, in the dense brush country of Texas, a horse had to have quick responses and moves to follow and anticipate a calf's, or steer's, every move in order to put his rider in the right position for a short-distance rope throw, once a rare gap in the brush was found. In the more open country of California, the horse was taught to line the rider up for a clean longer rope throw.

The working cowboy, who is not going to change his saddle every time he cuts or ropes, or does any other job, uses a general stock saddle that suits him, his horse and his work best. In more recent years, however, styles and fashions have changed or been modified to suit all today's competitive disciplines, which are widely supported, particularly in the United States but also increasingly in Europe and the United Kingdom. Reining (the Western equivalent of a dressage test) has now become an Olympic sport.

TO FIT It is vitally important that the Western saddle fits the horse well and helps the rider to attain good balance. The width of the saddle bars is very important to the fit. The bars are the two long horizontal pieces of the Western tree that rest on the horse's back on either side of the spine. They are the weight-bearing surfaces and also support and stabilize the fork and cantle. The whole surface of the bars must lie flat against the horse's sides to bear the weight correctly and, to ensure this happens, different bar widths are available to fit differing conformation. The bar widths are categorized thus: regular (about

parts of a Western saddle

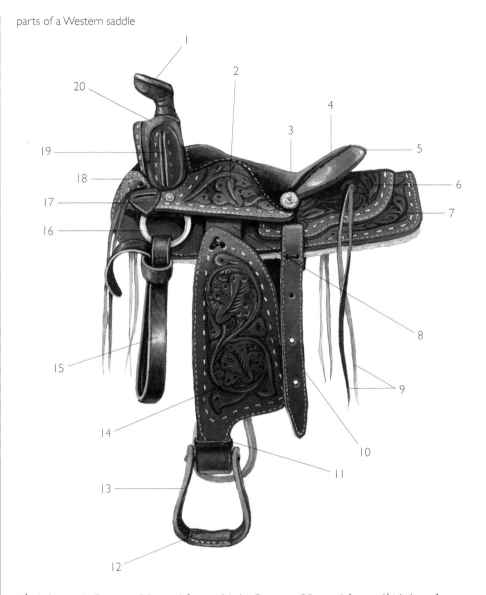

1. horn
2. side jockey
3. seat
4. cantle
5. cheyenne roll
6. back jockey
7. skirt
8. stirrup leather (under fender)
9. saddle strings
10. back (flank) cinch billet
11. stirrup leather keeper
12. stirrup tread
13. stirrup
14. fender
15. latigo
16. front rigging ring
17. latigo carrier
18. front jockey
19. swell
20. fork

5½ in); semi-Quarter Horse (about 6 in); Quarter Horse (about 6½ in) and Arabian or Morgan (about 6¾ in). It is important that the horse has the correct width fitting; if the saddle is too wide it will bear down on his withers and back, and if it is too narrow it will pinch the horse and restrict his movement. As you look at the saddle from the side, it must appear level. If a rider is in the saddle, they must neither look like they are riding uphill nor downhill.

Pads and/or blankets are usually placed under Western saddles and they must be kept clean and free of any irritant that could make the horse sore.

When saddling the horse, the Western saddle can be placed a little forward on the horse's back and then slid back into its correct position, or the horn can be grasped and the saddle gently shaken back into place. The hairs under the saddle will then lie flat in the direction of growth. There must be 2 in clearance at the withers – with the weight of a rider in the saddle – and when you look down the gullet, it should clear the horse's spine all the way through. Make sure that any saddle pad and/or blanket is pulled up into the gullet to avoid pressure on the withers.

With the cinching (girthing) system on a Western saddle there are five 'rigging' positions, and the cinch (girth) attaches to the rigging ring which is either in the tree or the skirt. The positions are: centre fire, $^5/_8$, $^3/_4$, $^7/_8$ or full (Spanish or rim fire). 'Centre fire' is in the middle of the saddle, 'full' is at the front of the saddle, and the remaining three come in between. If the saddle has one of the three

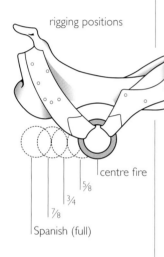

rigging positions

centre fire

$^5/_8$

$^3/_4$

$^7/_8$

Spanish (full)

forward rigging positions (full, $^7/_8$ or $^3/_4$), it will usually have both a front and back (flank) cinch – or, at least, provision for a back cinch (the back cinch stops the back of the saddle tipping up). With the two remaining positions $^5/_8$ and centre fire) a back cinch is not necessary. If both front and back cinches are used, a cinch connector strap is required to stop the back cinch from sliding back too far. This strap attaches to D rings in the centre of both the front and back cinches.

Traditionally, the Western cinches (girths) were attached to the rigging ring on the nearside by long leather straps (latigos) which were wrapped around the rigging ring and the cinch ring and tied in a knot similar to a Windsor knot. Most modern cinches have buckles and the latigos have holes punched in them to take the buckle tongues. On the offside, cinches are buckled to billet straps.

With a cinch in the full, $^7/_8$ or $^3/_4$ positions, it is most important that the cinch does not rub the horse behind the elbow. If a cinch is in the $^5/_8$ or centre fire position, rubbing here is not so likely to be a problem. To make sure that the cinch lies correctly, there must be an equal distance between the ends of the cinch and the saddle on both sides, when the cinch is tightened. There will then be an equal pull on both sides, the saddle will sit straight, and the D rings for the attachment of the breastcollar and cinch connector strap will also be centrally placed.

Cinches are available in different lengths and widths to suit all sizes and specific requirements of conformation and use.

Roping saddle

The roping saddle is a very substantially made saddle, both structurally and weight-wise, it usually weighs anywhere between 33 and 55 lb to stand up to the constant strain that a heavy animal on the end of the rope puts on the saddle roping saddle

structure. The horn is large to accommodate the rope and is usually 3 in high and often 3 in in diameter as well. Some ropers prefer rawhide-covered horns or will themselves put strips of rubber around the horn to prevent the rope from slipping. The roping saddle is designed not to hinder the roper who is in and out of the saddle frequently. The swells at the front of the saddle are narrow and the cantle at the back is usually low so the rider can leave the saddle fast. The narrowness of the swells also means that the rope will not get caught on them, as it might on a saddle with wider swells. The stirrups are very heavy with a wide tread so that they hang straight down and do not follow the foot in a rapid dismount.

Cutting saddle

The cutting saddle has a slightly flatter, bigger seat and has a thinner, longer saddle horn because in the cutting competitions the rider is allowed to hold the saddle horn. The stirrups have good forward swing and the oxbow stirrup is usually used which has a very narrow, rounded stirrup tread that tucks up in to the gap of the rider's boot between the heel and the sole. This is a dangerous style of stirrup for everyday riding as it is not easy to detach the foot in an emergency. The saddle is designed to help the rider remain balanced as the horse rapidly follows each movement of the animal he is working.

cutting saddle

Reining saddle

The reining saddle is designed for reining work and reining competitions. Reining competitions are the Western dressage tests. They comprise set patterns of movement and horse and rider perform a set test. Each movement is marked individually to build a final score, and the judge also awards marks for willingness, obedience and accuracy. The stirrups have a lot of forward swing to allow the rider to execute in particular the sliding stop; the legs swinging forward give the horse the cue to stop. The saddle itself allows the rider freedom of movement to use the body to guide the horse through the exercises.

reining saddle

show saddle

Show or equitation saddle

The show or equitation saddle is designed for show or parade, and would be used for the competition disciplines of Western Riding, Western Trail and Western Pleasure. The style of the saddle remains the same but the decoration varies dramatically; fashion plays a big part in the decoration and colouring of show saddles. Plainer versions of the same style could be used for everyday pleasure riding. The stirrups hang down straight and have very little forward swing because the rider will not have to slide the legs forward as dramatically as is required by some of the other Western disciplines. The saddle is designed to help the rider adopt a slightly more upright elegant pose. The horn is small and low as it is only for show and not used in these classes. The cantle is usually high and the seat deep.

show saddle

Barrel racing saddle

The barrel racing saddle is a much lighter cut-down version of the other Western saddles. Barrel racing is a speed and agility event and the saddle is light and has shorter skirts to allow the horse more freedom of movement. The seat is usually built to hold the rider well in position to allow upper body central weight change to encourage but not hamper the horse.

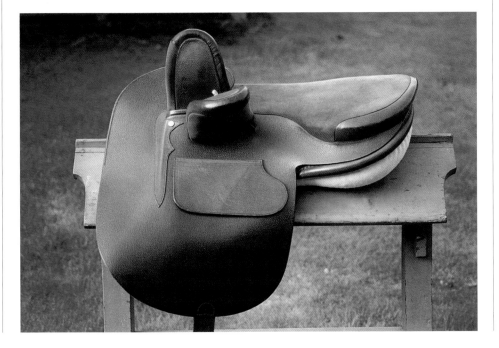

barrel racing saddle

Side-saddles

Many saddles currently in use were made between 1850 and 1939 but side-saddles are still being made today in the traditional way. Some older saddles have a distinct dip in the seat, making it difficult for the rider to keep her weight poised forward, although the straight-seated saddle is thought by many to tip the rider forward too far. Modern saddles are usually made with a slight dip of around 6 mm and this appears to provide the most comfortable position.

Most side-saddles are made of leather with a serge lining covered in linen – fabric being easier to restitch than leather after reflocking. Leather-lined side-saddles are less frequently encountered. Occasionally you might come across a side-saddle conventional in all other respects but having a detachable felt pad

a modern side-saddle

Nearside

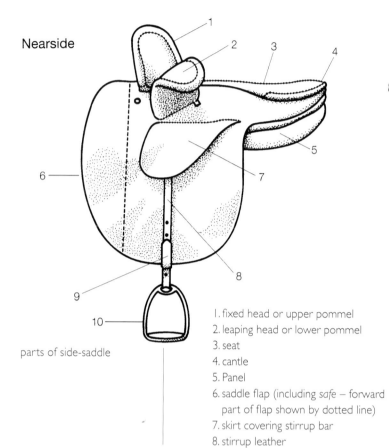

Offside

parts of side-saddle

1. fixed head or upper pommel
2. leaping head or lower pommel
3. seat
4. cantle
5. Panel
6. saddle flap (including *safe* – forward part of flap shown by dotted line)
7. skirt covering stirrup bar
8. stirrup leather

9. keeper covering hook for adjusting length of leather
10. stirrup iron
11. balance or Sefton girth
12. balance or Sefton girth
13. underside of *safe* viewed from offside
14. leather tab with hook to secure offside flap
15. girth

right serge-lined side-saddle with linen covering

far right leather-lined side-saddle

instead of the panel. this is known as a Wykeham pad and was intended for use on a horse or pony with a wide back.

The seat and the pommels of a side-saddle are usually covered with doeskin which affords the rider a better grip than leather. The length of the saddle must be the correct length for the rider. If the seat is too short or too long, the rider will be disadvantaged by having to sit behind, or in advance of, the correct (and most comfortable) part of the saddle.

seat and pommels of a side-saddle covered with doeskin

The upper pommel is fixed and supports the rider's right leg. It is important that the curve and position of this pommel is appropriate for the length of the rider's thigh, and places the right thigh bone diagonally across the seat of the saddle. If the rider has to twist her body round in order to reach the pommel, she will never achieve a secure, comfortable and straight seat. Many older saddles were made-to-measure for their owners so it is vital to consider the length of the seat and the position of the upper pommel when buying a second-hand side-saddle.

The lower pommel is known as the leaping head because the left leg can be pushed up into the curve for extra security in an emergency and when jumping. Leaping heads unscrew and are made with a reverse thread. Some are adjustable, enabling the leaping head to be moved to suit the leg position of the rider.

Conventional side-saddles seat the rider to the left, but it is possible to find an 'off-side' saddle where the rider sits to the right. There is even a saddle made with reversible pommels whereby both the top pommel and the leaping head can be unscrewed and set on the other side.

an off-side side-saddle

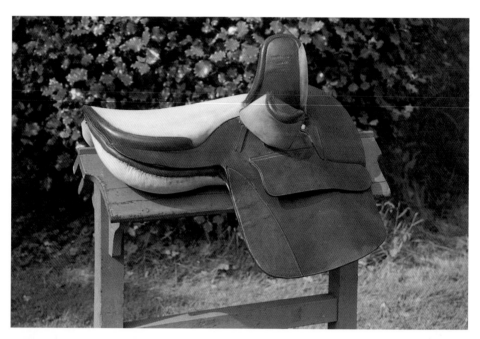

below side-saddle with reversible pommels

below right same saddle with pommels reversed

TO FIT All side-saddles have cutaway fronts and should have generous flocking, providing a wide and flat bearing surface on either side of a deep gullet. A good side-saddle will fit a variety of horses and exactly the same principles apply to the fitting of side-saddles as to astride saddles. Viewed from the back the saddle should sit absolutely straight and there should be good clearance of the horse's spine. A saddle that is too narrow for the horse will sit too high at the withers, pinch the horse and cause the rider to slip backwards. Alternatively, if the saddle is too wide for the horse it will move around, scalding the horse's back, and causing both horse and rider to feel extremely insecure.

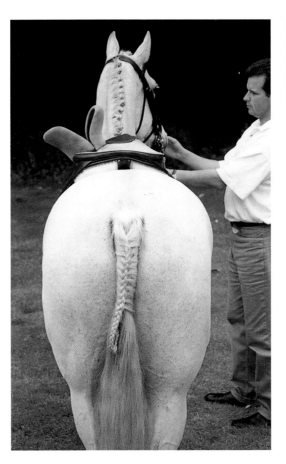

well-fitting side-saddle showing good clearance of the horse's spine

12. Care of Your Tack

Cleaning

For safety and durability all leatherwork should be regularly cleaned and nourished. Leather that has been excessively wet or dried out by direct heat or is kept in a very dry, warm environment gets very hard and brittle. Very wet leather should always be dried out naturally.

Although it is easier and quicker to wipe over and then lightly soap your tack without undoing all the buckles, try to take your tack completely apart at least once a month so you can thoroughly clean, and then apply leather soap or preparation to, the important buckle areas.

First of all you need to clean any dried sweat, grease or saliva from all your leatherwork. This should be done with clean warm water and a cloth or sponge. It is important that you wet the leather only enough to clean it; do not soak it in water. If you are using saddle soap use a second barely damp sponge or cloth. (If the sponge or cloth is too wet it will make your saddle soap lather and only coat

cleaning the underside of a saddle with a sponge

your tack very thinly with wet foamy soap, which will not supple the leather at all.) Rub the cloth or sponge in the saddle soap continuously until you have a thick sticky layer on it then carefully wipe it over your leatherwork so that it too now has a sticky layer of soap on it.

If you are using a leather preservative or preparation you may not need to wet your cloth or sponge but do make sure you apply enough to actually do the leatherwork some good. Examine your tack carefully as you are cleaning it; look for any signs of wear and check that all the stitching is sound. Pay particular attention to the underside of all your leatherwork as this is raw leather with no finish on it so this is the side that will really benefit from dressings and soaps that feed the leather.

Bridlework

The areas most susceptible to wear on a bridle are the rein and cheekpiece billets or buckles that attach to the bit. The bit must be removed regularly and the billets and buckle areas cleaned thoroughly. Dried saliva and food remnants are particular enemies of this part of the bridlework. If the reins are sewn onto the bit, great attention must be paid to cleaning and checking the stitching of the rein loops. Check all buckles and stitching.

Saddles

Firstly, as with the bridlework, clean your saddle with a sponge or cloth and warm water making sure all the grease and sweat is cleaned off. As you are cleaning, check your saddle for signs of wear and tear or stitching that is undone. Check in particular the girth straps; after a lot of use they can stretch and the holes that you buckle your girth to can get elongated. It is important that these are well maintained and replaced when worn. It is very important that you do not excessively wet or oil the seat of your saddle. If the seat is made of pigskin, the oil will soak right through the seat and into the webbing below then, when you sit on the saddle, the oil will seep back onto the seat of your breeches.

Storing Saddlery

Long-term storage

If you are storing your tack over a period of time you should:

1. Take it apart.

2. Clean it thoroughly with warm water and a damp cloth or sponge.

3. Either lightly coat it in oil or a leather preserving gel, including the buckles.

4. Wrap each piece in newspaper to protect from mildew. Put a layer of paper over the top of the saddle and a layer underneath inside the storage bag.

5. Store in proper bridle and saddle storage bags or in heavy sports bags.

6. Store in a dry moderately warm place free from vermin.

Everyday storage

Saddles should always be stored on a proper saddle rack. When taking a saddle to a show or event, carry it in a saddle-shaped, well-padded storage bag and stand it up on its knee rolls and pommel. Bridles can be hung up on a hook or stored in a bag.

13. Saddle Accessories

Seat Savers

Seat savers are a comfortable pad for the rider to sit on. The best ones are either sheepskin or well-designed gel pads. They must fit well and not move around on the seat of your saddle. The best fittings are small straps that go under the skirts of the saddle and a long elasticated strap that goes from the front to the back of the saddle under the gullet.

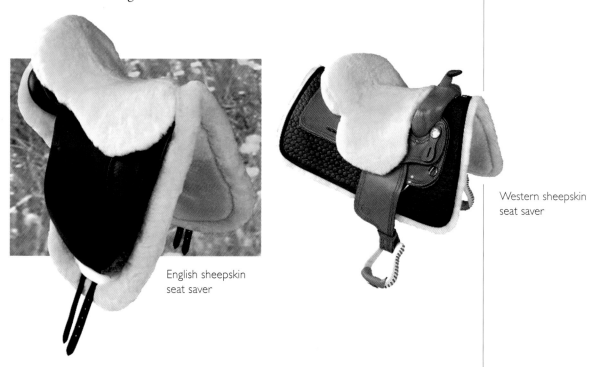

English sheepskin seat saver

Western sheepskin seat saver

Cruppers

A crupper is a strap that helps to keep the saddle from sliding forward onto the withers of a small pony. It could also be used to stabilize a roller when lungeing or long reining to make it more secure on the horse's back. The roller or saddle will need an additional D ring at the back on the top of the roller or just under the top edge of the saddle cantle to which the crupper is attached. It is very important that the dock part of the crupper is kept very supple as the skin under the horse's tail is extremely sensitive and gets rubbed very easily; keep a careful check on this area. If your horse is not used to a crupper, introduce it in the stable in a controlled environment so that the horse has time to get used to the unfamiliar feel before you use it outside as you work.

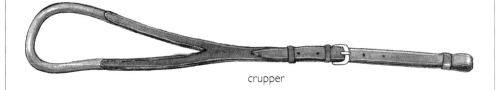

crupper

Girth Sleeves

These sleeves come in materials ranging from sheepskin and wool mixes to nylon simulated fur and even breathable plastic. The sleeve goes around the girth to protect the horse's skin from the material of the girth. Some horses have very sensitive skin and need quite a bit of protection to prevent their tack and equipment from rubbing them.

ordinary girth sleeve

dressage girth sleeve

Girth Guards

Girth guards are small shaped pieces of leather that slot onto the girth pulls or straps just under the saddle flap. When the girth is tight enough, the girth guard is pulled down over the buckles of the girth to prevent the buckles wearing away at the underside of the saddle flap.

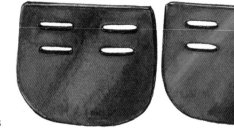

girth guards

14. Stirrup Irons and Stirrup Leathers

Stirrup Irons

Stirrup irons must fit the foot well for safety reasons. Check that the iron fits properly by placing your foot in the iron when it is on the floor. You should have half an inch either side of your boot when you have the ball of your foot on the iron. Then, rock your foot back on to the heel as you tip the stirrup iron forward with your hand; your toe should clear the top of the iron. This simulates a rider falling off and the foot leaving the stirrup. If the toe does not clear the top of the stirrup a rider could be dragged. Stirrup irons are measured across the inside span.

Although called 'irons' they are no longer made of iron. These days they should be made of good quality stainless steel and be heavy so that if you lose a stirrup the iron's own weight will make it drop down to the end of the stirrup leather and make it easier for the rider to find the iron again.

English hunting irons
These stirrup irons have a flat side and a substantial footplate. This is a heavy iron designed to hang at the bottom of the stirrup leather returning there quickly dropped by its own weight if the foot comes out of the iron.

Fillis irons
These irons have a round side and are designed to look more elegant from the side. They are a little deeper in the footplate than ordinary English irons but just as substantial.

English hunting irons

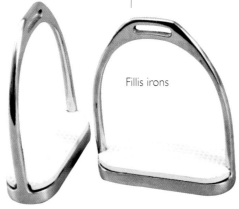

Fillis irons

Bent-leg or Simplex irons

The outside branch of this iron is bent forward to act as a safety feature; should the rider fall from the horse it is easier for the foot to come cleanly out of the iron. This is a good safety iron for adult weights.

Peacock irons

This safety iron is more suitable for the weight of a child because it does not have an outside branch and is prone to bending, which makes the footplate tip down to the outside. The outside branch is replaced with a strong rubber band which will stretch or come away to prevent a child's leg being caught in the stirrup.

bent-leg irons

peacock irons

Race irons

Race irons are very small and very light so they will not add a lot of weight to the jockeys' equipment during weigh-in.

Western stirrups

Western stirrups were originally made of wood and either left as plain wood or bound in rawhide or laced leather. The modern wooden stirrups are often bound in steel and, in addition, might have a laced or braided rawhide or leather covering. Stainless steel and manmade materials such as polyethylene are also used.

There are two main styles of Western stirrup: the oxbow and the visalia. The former has narrow side pieces and tread, and the whole stirrup is curved, or rounded. The latter has a flatter wider tread and wider side pieces. There are a number of variations on these styles, and the choice of stirrup depends on the rider's preference for size, shape, the job to be done and decoration. The requirements of the working cowboy will differ from those of the rodeo, pleasure or show rider. Some show stirrups are made of highly decorated stainless steel, while others have inlaid silver decoration.

oxbow stirrup

visalia-style stirrup

Side-saddle irons

Before the advent of quick-release stirrup-leather safety bars, a conventional leather was threaded through a plain fixed roller beneath the skirt of the saddle and the safety of the rider depended upon a safety stirrup. These were rather

swing-release safety stirrup

cumbersome and looked like a stirrup within a stirrup, having either a swing-release mechanism or a hinge designed to come apart in the event of a fall. When safety bars with quick-release mechanisms were introduced it became possible to use a plain stirrup iron.

Stirrup Treads

Rubber stirrup treads give a rider better grip and prevent the foot slipping out of the stirrup, particularly in wet weather.

English hunting stirrup treads
The English hunting stirrup treads are designed specifically to fit onto the flat-sided English hunting stirrup iron.

Fillis stirrup treads
The Fillis treads are designed specifically to fit onto the round-sided Fillis stirrup iron. You have to be careful that you buy the correct treads, as ordinary treads will not fit this deep iron. Fillis treads have a piece cut out of the side to accommodate the side of the iron.

Wedge treads
Not only do these treads provide grip but, because they are, as the name suggests, wedge-shaped, they also help the rider's foot to stay in a correct position.

Stirrup Leathers

Best English leathers
These leathers are made of the best quality leather which results in a supple and safe stirrup leather. This quality leather comes from the hide back.

Hunting leathers
Hunting leathers are made of a heavier gauge of leather than everyday leathers to ensure you survive the rigours of a day's hunting.

Showing leathers

These leathers are made of the best quality English leather but are very narrow to complement the fine bridlework and elegance of showing saddlery.

Buffalo leathers

Made from buffalo hide, these leathers are very strong, never break, need little maintenance and are used commonly on polo saddles. The downside is that buffalo leather stretches considerably.

showing leathers

buffalo leathers

Western leathers

Unlike English leathers, Western leathers are attached directly to the tree, either through a slot in the bar or in a groove on the inside of the bar. The leather is either a single strap with a separate fender (the wide leather strap that covers the stirrup leather), or the leather and fender can be made from one piece of leather.

At one time the leathers were laced which meant that, in order to adjust them, the lacing had to be undone and then relaced once the adjustment to the required length had been made. Today leathers are more commonly adjusted by means of either single-tongued or double-tongued buckles, or the pronged 'quick-change' buckles.

Side-saddle leathers and safety bars

Modern side-saddle stirrup leathers are not fixed to the saddle via a roller as they used to be. Today the leathers are attached to safety bars with quick-release mechanisms that ensure the rider's safety in the event of a fall. The leather is stitched to a fitting that attaches to, usually, one of three types of safety bar: Champion & Wilton, Mayhew or Whippy, or Owen.

Champion & Wilton safety bar

stirrup leather and attachment

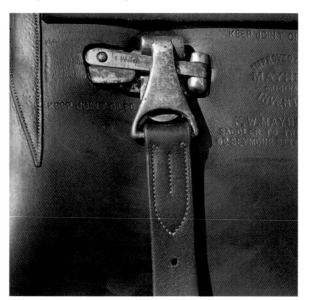

Mayhew or Whippy safety bar

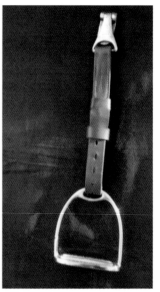

stirrup leather and attachment

Owen safety bar

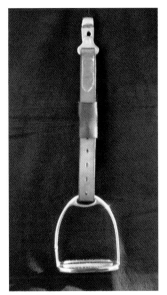

stirrup leather and attachment

Side-saddle leathers have a hook and hole method of adjustment, which is situated further down the leather than on an astride-saddle leather. The hook is covered by a leather sleeve to prevent the rider's leg being rubbed.

15. Girths

Synthetic Girth

This is a modern, very practical, girth usually 3 in wide and straight cut, i.e. the same width all the way along, and manufactured in a variety of colours. It is an easy-maintenance product. Made in a variety of lengths from approximately 30 in for small ponies to 58 in for large horses.

synthetic girth

Cord Girth

This traditional girth is made up of cords laid side by side and bound with cotton to keep the cords straight and together. The latest versions of this girth are made of a very soft thick cord which holds its shape very well and evenly distributes the pressure over a wide area which is much more comfortable for the horse.

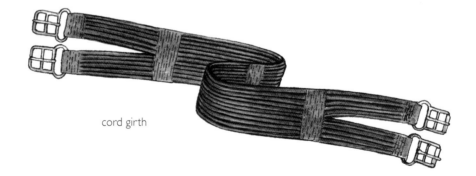

cord girth

Vagabond

This is a very soft, shaped girth designed to follow the contours of the horse's chest and to allow plenty of room behind the horse's elbow. A girth rub behind the elbow of a sensitive-skinned horse can develop into a girth gall. By shaping the girth and making it narrower in this area you reduce the likelihood of a gall. The Vagabond is usually made of bag hide, which is very soft leather.

Balding

The Balding girth is another shaped girth, designed to be narrower just behind the horse's elbows to help to prevent girth galls in this vulnerable area. The narrowing is achieved by the leather being split into three and plaited. As it does not have soft edges like the Vagabond and the Atherstone girths it is important that this girth is kept soft and very supple.

Atherstone

The Atherstone girth is a soft folder-leather girth designed, again, to be narrower just behind the horse's elbows to help to prevent girth galls. Because the leather is folded, both edges of the girth are rounded for comfort.

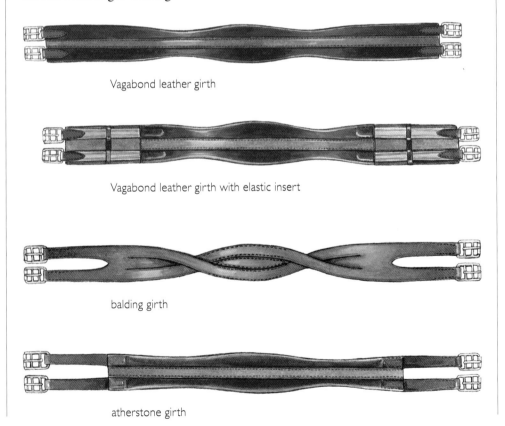

Vagabond leather girth

Vagabond leather girth with elastic insert

balding girth

atherstone girth

Leather Stud-guard Girth

This is a very wide leather girth. As a jumping horse folds up his front feet to jump a fence, he can sometimes fold his legs up so tightly into the chest that he actually cuts himself with his own jumping studs. This girth protects the chest area to prevent cutting and bruising.

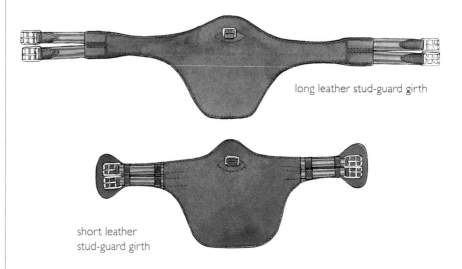

long leather stud-guard girth

short leather stud-guard girth

Overgirth

Overgirths can be made of either leather or webbing and fit over the top of the saddle to make it doubly secure when showjumping, riding over cross-country fences or playing polo. The saddle is girthed up as normal and then the overgirth is put on over the saddle, like a surcingle.

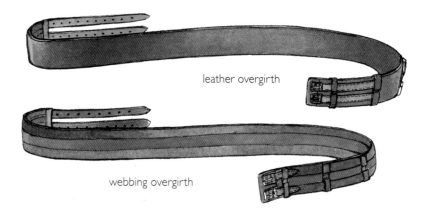

leather overgirth

webbing overgirth

Dressage Girth

Most dressage saddles and some jumping saddles have girth pulls. These are long girth straps which buckle low down behind the horse's shoulder which reduces the bulk under the rider's leg.

leather dressage girth

leather dressage girth
with elastic end

Cinch

Traditionally, 'string' or cord Western cinches (girths) were made of mane hair but today this style of cinch is more likely to be made of mohair or rayon. These cinches are very similar to the English cord girths. The width of the cinch depends upon the number of cords placed side by side: the narrowest having about 15 cords and the widest approximately 30 cords. Web is also a popular material for cinches and usually has a fleece or felt lining. Back cinches are, as a rule, made of leather. Cinches are available in different lengths and widths to suit all horses and ponies.

cord front cinch

Side-saddle Girth and Balance Strap

A conventional three-fold leather girth is often used with a side-saddle. A short balance strap is sometimes stitched onto the girth approximately one third of the length along the girth from the buckles end. It is often said that the perfectly

below left short balance strap

below right lifting the off-side flap to enable the girths to be tightened whilst mounted, showing a full balance strap and a side-saddle girth with a surcingle or overgirth on top; the rider is holding a hook attached to a band of elastic which fastens onto the overgirth and keeps the flap in position.

fitting side-saddle needs no balance strap. Nevertheless, most saddles have provision for them. The balance strap (or Sefton girth) helps to keep the saddle in position. A flat leather side-saddle girth has stitched keepers to allow for a slender secondary or surcingle girth, which is stitched to the flap on the nearside, and a full balance strap. The latter is attached to a strap set just above the rear panel of the saddle between the offside flap and the back of the saddle. It joins the main girth under the belly and buckles onto a strap set in front of the main girth straps on the nearside.

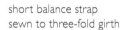

short balance strap
sewn to three-fold girth

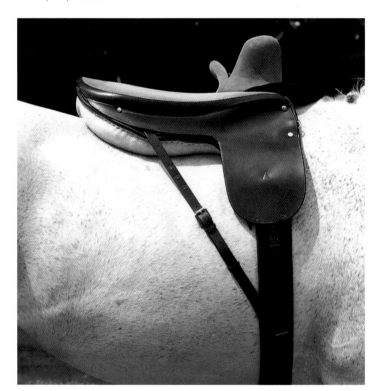

Girth Size Guide

If you are buying a new girth, take an old girth that fits your horse well into the saddlers with you so that you have an accurate size comparison.

This size chart gives an approximate guide to girth sizes for different horse and pony heights. I always get mixed up with the conversion of inches to centimetres so the chart opposite also gives this conversion.

balance strap shown in front of the main girth (note surcingle or overgirth stitched to the saddle flap)

some saddles have girth straps mounted on top of the off-side flap (note attachment for balance strap

Horses height in hands	Girth size in inches	Girth size in centimetres
10.0	30–32	75–80
10.2	32–34	80–85
11.0	34–36	85–90
11.2	36–38	90–95
12.0	38–40	95–100
12.2	40–42	100–105
13.0	42–44	105–110
13.2	44–46	110–115
14.0	46–48	115–120
14.2	46–48	115–120
15.0	48–50	120–125
15.2	50–52	125–130
16.0	50–52	125–130
16.2	52–54	130–135
17.0	54–56	135–140
17.2	56–58	140–145

16. Numnahs, Saddle Squares, Saddle Pads and Gel Pads

Most of us these days use some sort of numnah or saddle square under our saddles, whether it is a light cotton quilt just to keep the underneath of the saddle clean, or something much thicker for a specific purpose. A word of advice: when washing something that is in close contact with your horse's skin for long periods of time, and where heat is generated, make sure the item is washed in mild detergent and rinsed well because some horses are allergic to harsh soaps, just as some humans are.

Numnahs

A numnah is a pad in the shape of the saddle and comes in a variety of different materials and thicknesses. The two most common numnahs are the general purpose numnah which is forward cut to fit the shape of the general purpose saddle flap and the dressage numnah which is much straighter cut to follow the line of the straight thigh roll of a dressage saddle. You can colour coordinate with the bandages and numnah in one colour and the binding around the numnah's edge in a constrasting colour. Generally, however, competition numnahs are white, black or brown.

TO FIT The numnah must be slightly bigger than the saddle it is to go under to ensure that the saddle does not press down on the seams of the numnah and

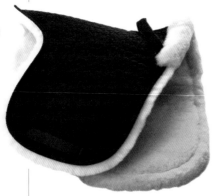

quilted dressage numnah with all-wool lining

general purpose numnah with wool lining the bearing surface

cause a pressure point on the horse's back. As you place the saddle over the numnah you must lift the numnah up into the gullet of the saddle before girthing up so that there is no pressure on the horse's spine. The strap at the front of the numnah loops around, and is secured by, one of the girth pulls under the flap on each side before the saddle is girthed up and the girth passes through a loop at the bottom of the numnah just under the panel of the saddle.

Specialist Numnahs

Show numnah

Show numnahs are cut very straight to accommodate the shape of a show saddle and are designed to just cover the undersurface of the saddle so that they lie very neatly under the saddle and do not stick out and detract from the overall appearance of the animal or cover the all important shoulder area. Show numnahs should always be brown or a very dark colour to match the brown show tack.

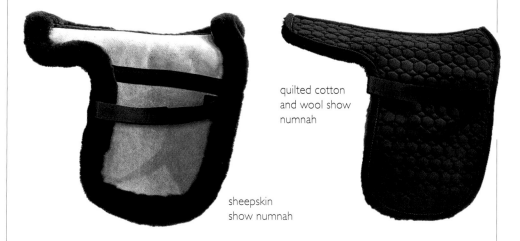

quilted cotton and wool show numnah

sheepskin show numnah

Jumping numnah

To allow for the large knee roll on a jumping saddle, the jumping numnah is very forward cut. The numnah shown is a half jumping numnah. Some of the close-contact jumping saddles are very narrow over the waist, so the less bulk between the horse and the saddle the better.

half jumping numnah

Half numnah

The half numnah is designed to sit under the bearing surface of the saddle so that, for the horse's comfort, the saddle sits on a shaped pad but the rider has less bulk under the leg.

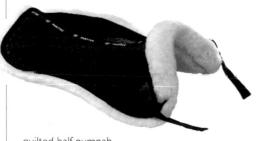

sheepskin half numnah

quilted half numnah

Side-saddle numnah

The side-saddle has a very wide bearing surface which evenly distributes the rider's weight but does not cover both sides of the horse, this specially designed numnah allows the horse to be comfortable while the look of the saddle retains its elegance.

side-saddle numnah

Saddle Squares

This type of saddle pad is designed, just as the numnah is, to fit under the saddle to either keep the saddle clean or to afford extra padding for the horse in differing degrees. Instead of being saddle shaped these pads are almost square. Saddle squares designed for general purpose or jumping saddles are cut slightly forward at the front and saddle squares to go under dressage saddles are almost completely straight at the front. With the latter shape, more square is seen and it is, therefore, used for either colour coordination purposes or for initials to be put on the corner of the square. Dressage competitors can

dressage saddle square

general purpose saddle square

have their competition number pouches sewn onto the corner of the square so that they can display the numbers for each class.

TO FIT The saddle square is fitted in exactly the same way as a numnah.

Specialist Saddle Squares

Western saddle square
This square fits under the very wide bearing surfaces of the Western saddle. Normally these pads are very thick and well padded to keep the horse comfortable during long hours under saddle.

Endurance saddle square
The endurance saddle square is very well cut, shaped and padded to keep the horse comfortable during the long hours that the endurance saddle is worn. It also has pockets so that small pieces of essential equipment can be carried.

Race saddle square
This is for race exercise saddles and is reversible: you can either have the wool side or the cotton quilted side next to the horse.

Western saddle square

endurance saddle square

race saddle square

Back Pads

There are dozens of back pads on the market and the most important points to remember are: they must be sufficiently thick to actually be of some use; they must be of good quality. A poor-quality pad will deteriorate when washed or in day-to-day use and spread the bearing load unevenly leading to pressure points or sores on the horse's back, thus causing the sort of trouble they are designed to prevent.

quilted and wool back pad

TO FIT They must be contoured so that they fit very well and they must be shaped enough to be pulled well up into the gullet so there is no downward pressure onto the spine.

Gel Pads

Gel pads should be flexible and cut to fit. If you squeeze the gel pad between your thumbnail and your index fingernail, the pad should be thick enough not to allow your fingernails to meet. To extend the life of a gel pad it is best not to have the pad directly next to the horse to reduce the amount of times it has to be washed. Place the pad over a light quilted square to extend its life.

gel pad

TO FIT They must be pliable so that they fit very well and if they are not cut into a shape to fit up into the gullet of the saddle, they must be pliable enough to be pulled well up into the gullet so there is no downward pressure onto the spine.

Driving-saddle Pads

Although a driving saddle is relatively small, it can still cause pressure and sore places. A driving-saddle pad is, therefore, essential for sensitive-skinned horses. The driving-saddle pad shown is actually under a lungeing roller to show it more clearly.

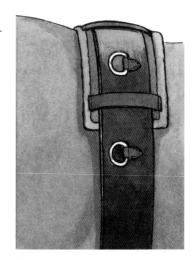

TO FIT The pad has Velcro fastenings that fasten the pad securely to the driving saddle to stop it slipping: one fastening under the gullet and one each side of the pad. It should be placed under the driving saddle and pulled well up into the gullet of the saddle before the Velcro is fastened and before the pad is girthed up.

driving saddle pad

Riser Pads

Riser pads are dense foam pads shaped so that they fit neatly under the bearing surface of the saddle and up into the gullet so that no pressure is brought to bear directly onto the horse's spine. Riser pads provide the means for a slight adjustment that can make a horse more comfortable, but they should not be used just to make a badly made saddle fit a horse. They have three different degrees of thickness and uses.

TO FIT The pad should be placed under the saddle so that the saddle fits comfortably in the middle of the pad and does not overlap the pad. It should fit well up into the gullet of the saddle. As this is a dense foam pad, the horse does tend to sweat under it if it is placed directly next to the skin so it would be better fitted over a light quilted numnah or saddle square. Make sure all the layers are well pulled up into the gullet of the saddle before the saddle is girthed up.

Ordinary riser pad

The ordinary riser is the same thickness all the way along the pad and is designed to give even comfortable padding under the whole bearing surface of the saddle.

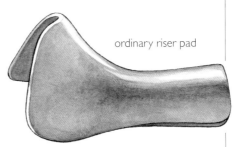

ordinary riser pad

Front riser pad

This is the same thickness as the ordinary riser but has extra padding at the front so that the saddle is lifted a little at the front.

Back riser pad

The back riser has the same dense padding all the way along but extra at the back in order to lift the saddle at the back.

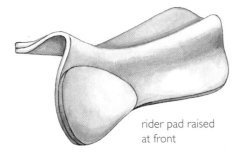

rider pad raised
at front

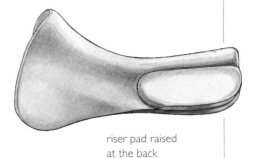

riser pad raised
at the back

Poly Pad

This rectangular pad comes in several thicknesses and is very easy to maintain as the outer is cotton and the inner is washable wadding. Designed without loops or fittings to attach them to the saddle, they do not move if fitted properly and pulled well up into the gullet of the saddle. They come in various colours and bindings so they can be co-ordinated with personal and team colours.

TO FIT It is very important that the pad is fitted correctly. Place it on the horse's back and slide it into position from front to back in the direction of the horse's coat growth. Place the saddle on top so that there is approximately 3 in of pad showing at the front and 2 in showing at the back of the saddle. Then hold the pad with one hand at the front over the horse's spine and one hand at the back and lift the pad right up into the gullet of the saddle so that there is a gap over the horse's spine, then girth up the saddle as normal.

poly pad

Western Pads and Blankets

The traditional felt pads and wool blankets, particularly the Navajo blankets, are still available and popular, but modern materials such as acrylic and polyester are now also used for pads. In addition, shock-absorbing and protector pads are now

Western pad

Navajo-style blanket

used in the Western field, as are shaped pads; barrel-racing pads, for example, are cut down to reduce the weight on a horse's back when he is trying to achieve the fastest time he can.

TO FIT Place the pad or blanket forward on the horse's back and slide it back into place to ensure his hairs are lying the right way. Check to see that there is an equal amount of pad/blanket on both sides of the horse. When the saddle is in place, there should be about 2–3 in showing in front of the saddle. The saddle pad/blanket must be lifted into the gullet of the saddle.

Useful Addresses

Master Saddlers

The Society of Master Saddlers (UK) Ltd
Kettles Farm, Mickfield, Stowmarket, Suffolk, IP14 6BY

Saddles and English Bridlework

E. Jeffries and Sons Ltd
George Street, Walsall, West Midlands, WS1 1SD
Tel: 01922 642222 Email: Sales@ejeffries.co.uk

IV Horse
East Balthangie, Cuminestown, Turrif, Aberdeen, AB53 5XY

Quality Numnahs and Saddle Accessories

Mattes Equestrian
The Old Rectory Coach House, Calstock, Cornwall, PA18 9SF
Tel: 01458 259403 Email: Mattesuk@aol.com

KB Bridles

Albion Saddlemakers Co Ltd
Albion House, Bridgeman Street, Walsall, West Midlands, WS2 9PG
Tel: 01922 646320 Website: www.albion-saddlemakers.co.uk

Gloster and Restrainer Nosebands

Spalding Saddlery
Cliffords Farm, Ovington, Richmond, North Yorkshire, DL11 7DD
Tel: 01833 627210 Fax: 01833 627562

Myler Combination Bridles

Belstane Marketing Ltd
Shaws Barn, Atlow, Nr Ashbourne, Derbyshire, DE6 1NS
Tel: 01335 372600

BR Schooling Equipment

Bieman de Haas BV
PO Box 8, 6658 ZG Beneden-Leeuwen, Netherlands
Tel: (+31) 0487 597880 Fax: (+31) 0487 591070

Worcester Nosebands

Shires Equestrian Products
15 Southern Avenue, Leominster, Herefordshire, HR6 0QF
Tel: 01568 613600 Fax: 01568 613599

Side-pull Bridles and Be Nice Halters

The Western Department
Rookery Farm Equestrian, Shabbington, Aylesbury, Buckinghamshire,
HP18 9HF
Tel and Fax: 01844 201656

Western Saddlery

Smith Brothers, P O Box 2700, Denton, Texas 76207, USA.
Tel: (800) 433-5558 Email: sbrown@smithbros.com
Website: www.Smithbrothers.com

Index